essays and journalism

Philip Martin

The University of Arkansas Press
Fayetteville • 1997

01   00   99   98   97   5   4   3   2   1

Designed by Liz Lester

☺   The paper used in this publication meets the minimum
requirements of the American National Standard for Permanence of
Paper for Printed Library Materials Z39.48-1984.

Library of Congress Cataloging-in-Publication Data

Martin, Philip, 1958–
        The shortstop's son : essays and journalism / Philip Martin.
            p.   cm.
        Many of essays originally appeared in the Arkansas Democrat
gazette.
        ISBN 1-55728-483-0 (cloth : alk. paper). —ISBN 1-55728-484-9
        (pbk. : alk. paper)
        I. Title
        PN4874.M4826A25   1997
        814'.54—dc21   97–14766
                                                                    CIP

● *for my mother and for Karen* ●

acknowledgments

It would be vanity to suppose that this book could have come about without the help of a great many people, at least some of whom are likely to be slighted due to the author's imperfect memory and habit of distraction—to them I humbly apologize.

Among those I did not forget, I must thank my friends and sounding boards Bill Jones and Rufus Griscom; my ever-encouraging editor Griffin Smith jr., who delivered me from desert exile and brought me back to Arkansas; Paul Greenberg, who collaborated in that rescue mission, perhaps more than he realizes; Walter Hussman, the publisher of the *Arkansas Democrat-Gazette,* for caring about quality; Michael Lacey, the executive editor of *New Times* and an exemplar of excellence in journalism, no matter what his competitors say about him; Stanley Tiner, a magnificent newspaperman (and "conservative with a heart"); David Bodney, a writing friend; Deborah Laake, a role model; Matt Jones, who helped with the computer stuff; Rebecca Patterson, who helped me locate electronic copies of some of these pieces; Jack Schnedler, a fine editor and able advocate; Debbie Self and others at the University of Arkansas Press, for their patience and professionalism; Joe Riddle, a copy editor extraordinaire who saw many of these pieces naked; Ed Gray, in whose section of the newspaper many of the pieces first appeared; Stephen Buel, an old friend and co-conspirator; and all my colleagues at the *Arkansas Democrat-Gazette.*

Finally, I want to thank my love and best editor, Karen Martin.

contents

• *reports*

introduction

Liberators of Delight:
A Defense of Critics

Some years ago, I was asked to give a talk about the role of arts criticism in newspapers and magazines—a sort of "how-to-do-it-on-a-limited-budget" seminar. It's probable that those who asked me to speak would have liked something more organized and thought-through than the rant I ultimately delivered, which was, I'm afraid, far more valuable to my own education than it could have been helpful to them.

Not long after that, it was suggested to me in passing by Stephen Buel, the publisher of *Spectrum Weekly*, a lamentably defunct alternative newspaper published in Little Rock, Arkansas, that I write about the idea of cultural criticism—on how and why it occurs, on its uses and delights. This piece would address such issues as when and why good criticism is good, and why bad criticism ought to be recognized and avoided. This essay, and several of the others collected in this book, is the latest in a continuing series of arguments about popular culture and its uses that I have held with others and myself: Why should anyone care about this reputedly bloodless business? Why should anyone practice it? I have thought about it, though not for too long.

This piece is also meant as a kind of rant, for heart-seizing momentum is crucial to my philosophy of criticism, and I am ready to make my defense.

But first, let us hear from the formidable social critic Susan Sontag, who in 1964—twenty-six years before her name passed the lips of the brainy sprite in *Gremlins II*—issued a provocative essay entitled "Against Interpretation" that asserted,

> To interpret is to impoverish, to deplete the world—
> in order to set up a shadow world of "meanings" . . .
> In most modern circumstances, interpretation amounts

to the philistine refusal to leave the work of art alone. Real art has the capacity to make us nervous. By reducing the work of art to its content and then interpreting *that*, one tames the work of art. Interpretation makes art manageable, comfortable.

As Sontag suggests, it is not the job of cultural critics to make the world more comfortable. Neither is it their job to "explain what an artist had in mind" or what he or she "meant" when he or she came to make a work of art. Criticism can be better understood as a way of making intellectual use of the images and interstices of the world, of providing an alternate channel to passive, unthinking acceptance of the art barrage.

For it is a barrage. The larger, unavoidable part of this fusillade is what we might call pop culture—advertising, music, film, stage, genre fiction, television, bad poetry, political propagandizing, and some instances of visual art and literature as well as all the various, hybrid cross-media examples of imagery we encounter on a regular basis. Writing about art is itself, of course, part of the cultural avalanche, and as such is also deserving of scrutiny. There are good and bad critics, just as surely as there are good and bad artists. Crit-crit is coming, if it has not yet arrived; *Spy* magazine has made some early, bitchy forays into the field and the *Village Voice* is infamous for the internecine battles conducted by its stable of critics (still waiting for the cover blurbs— "Hoberman on Brown," "Christgau on Firth"). This would-be critic's sense of the *zeitgeist* is that people are becoming more and more interested in subjects entirely tangential to the core human experiences of eating, sleeping, and sex. Darwinism must require us to become more effete and specialized as we evolve toward cyberspace and beyond.

Critics, if they are competent, invite us to consider new uses for the images and sound patterns we see and hear; they sketch connections in the air. Ideally, they liberate fresh delight in art rather than eviscerate through exegesis. Critics ought not be tamers of art, though undoubtably that is how many of the dull ones see themselves—as lawgivers, truth diviners, arbiters of, if not taste, at least *fashion*.

Those critics suck. Yet there is some justice in that they almost always know they suck; they know they are miserable little hacks, dry-eyed and consumptive, impotent Ahabs before the Great White Wail of creation.

Criticism is valuable because pop culture is the very air we breathe (or, if you prefer, the polluted sluice through which we glittering fish must slide). It is not, as some of the professionally virtuous seem to think, something that happens to us; it is part of what we are. It envelops us, and those who would deny its importance are either stupid or afflicted by a sort of intellectual autism or both.

I know a woman of some years who imagines her mind refined and her upbringing genteel; she stipulates that she has never been inside a Wal-Mart or unwrapped a meal beneath the Golden Arches. How sad for her, even if she is not, as we all suspect, lying.

What other people create informs us about ourselves, even if all they have created is something for the rubes to purchase or something to make Aunt Lola blush. We are the Beast of Reason; and even the reason(s) for a pop band like the Red Hot Chili Peppers ought to intrigue us: Look at these whip-haired young men, their blank hateful stares, their tattoos and their wonderful crushing noise—who can resist being fascinated by such a strange tribe? Isn't it natural that people might want to crack this elaborate system, might want to get at a significance beyond that provided by a lyric sheet or an accountant's yellow pad?

Almost no one these days would suggest that the point (not the meaning, but the *point*) of many rock 'n' roll bands has little to do with their putative music—some of which can perhaps be duplicated by any five chemically stoked adolescents locked in a garage with the necessary equipment for long enough. ("We're not letting you out until you've finished the power ballad.")

No, what the Red Hot Chili Peppers are about, what rock 'n' roll is about, is a certain stance—the unregenerate pose. Rock 'n' roll music is just one component of the stance, the not-even-essential soundtrack. James Dean, the tone-deaf bongo player, was a rock star with his hands stuffed deep into the flimsy pockets of a red windbreaker, his forever young brow furrowed and his mouth set hard in that rebel sneer. A few years ago the disgraced, lip-synching duo Milli Vanilli just closed the circle, proving again the extraneous nature of music to rock stardom. No, they weren't musicians, but they were beautiful boys and they were in a very real way very much rock 'n' roll. The argument might be made that Milli Vanilli was a more subversive band than the Sex Pistols in a quaint, "Gimme Some Money" sort of way. Though the Red Hot Chili Peppers may play their instruments, they are no more or less legitimate than Milli Vanilli in this important respect: They—and truth be told, most rock bands, even the very good ones—are more like works of art—that is, things created—than creators of art. Perhaps the real artisans have always been the unseen executives who assemble and package rock groups, men like Maurice Starr and Rick Rubin and Colonel Tom Parker.

Social critics, to be successful, have to recognize the ultimate silliness of pop culture—and love it. What does critics in, what makes them bitter, is their insistence that pop market artifacts be genuine, sincere, and washed in the blood of earnestness. Rock music critics are possibly the worst at this, because most pop music is so simple and direct that criticism is superfluous. What is there to write about all but a few thoughtful and clever rock artists (Pete Townshend, Elvis Costello, Madonna, Richard Thompson, Paul Simon, Iggy Pop) except they play loud and look pretty and have lovely hair? Well, what does one say about the second album?

Yet rock music has a power that is only feebly echoed in all but the bravest rock criticism (people such as Lester Bangs, Greil Marcus, and Stanley Booth). And would anyone rather read about Prince than listen to him? Sadly, yes. Some rock-crit types. And, shudder, rock-crit wannabes.

Look, kids, you shouldn't want to become a critic—you should want to be a writer, or a guitar player, or a painter, or an architect, or a director. Criticism is what writers who are too lazy to be real reporters do to make a living. To be a real critic you have to be a real writer, and to be a real writer isn't all that easy. You want my job? *My* job?

Well, you'd better be willing to think and to write—to use all kinds of sentences, to give up the crutchy myth of synonyms, to be precise, and to be receptive to joy and pain; to know hawk from handsaw and camp from kitsch and sentimentality from sententiousness. Most of all, you'd better respect the glory of art.

Good art is like a benign drug, a passport to another kind

of consciousness. Art *does* possess the potential to effect change—biological and intellectual as well as social. But most art is second-rate. In fact, so much of it is second-rate that it almost goes without saying that a work is second rate—what a critic's real practical purpose is to identify the third-rate (what they call "pleasant," "humane," "skillfully assembled," etc.) or the fourth-rate ("competent"). The first-rate stuff takes care of itself; generally, it either rises to a certain level and goes no further (Flaubert, the folk singer T Bone Burnett) or else the artist dies penniless in some garrett and they discover the poor bastard's genius posthumously.

So pop criticism is silly because much of pop culture is silly. Imagine becoming an apologist for silly people with a rudimentary understanding of how to work a guitar or to set up a punch line or to manipulate light and film so as to make the bourgeois sob. Explicating such silliness is itself silly, dodgy work, and—for certain kinds of critics who specialize in writing about mass-market film, television, and music for general (i.e., postliterate) audiences—eventually soul destroying.

This is especially true when it is compounded by the psychic violence inflicted by the certain knowledge—verified by unpleasant letters and encounters in restaurants—that many people really do care about the musicians and the actors they hear on the radio and see on television. They imagine stretches of sincerity and dignity beneath the corrected, gleamy teeth and the glossy yards of hair. To them, the rock band Nelson and the icon Tom Cruise are forces for good, a beacon of comfort in an otherwise disturbing, uncomfortable world.

Critics snap on lights in a dark, filthy kitchen and generate skittering roaches—it is no wonder they are reviled.

I mean to defend critics here, but this is only a qualified defense. Critics *are* responsible for much of what is bad about art—some of them have bought into relativism and Paul de Man's deconstructivist techniques because it is fun to pretend that bad art is legitimate.

Yet it is hardly profound to notice that silly art can be fun, can offer diversion, can waste time pleasantly. It is also easy to hedge one's bets, to be oblique when one is unsure, and to temper harsh and generous opinions alike into sort of a blasé mush which trumpets to the world that one is erudite and sophisticated and can write like an angel with guts of steel, so what does it matter whether the little play was a good little play or a bad little play? Besides, some of the actors are one's friends, and, well, on deadline a formula is a nice, comfortable thing to slip into . . .

Good criticism is antidemocratic and judgmental. It believes in right and wrong, in worth and worthlessness. It is a trench against the invading shabbiness of thought; there is a culture war going on, and there is more than one front—the Jesse Helmses on the right flank and the relativists on the left, traitors in our midst and bloated blimps adorned with crockery (courtesy of the self-promoting Julian Schnabel) circling overhead. We're doomed, of course; the philistines will eventually overrun our positions, but there certainly must be a supernatural reward for those who perish with pure hearts, speaking for the indestructibility of beauty and the reality of the sublime.

reflections

A Murder Story

In the morning, when the police came, they found her apartment in disarray and a record still turning on the phonograph in an endless groove. A reporter could not resist noting the awful irony of the album title—it was *Killer on the Rampage* by the Jamaican pop star Eddy Grant.

The album contained a hit song, a one-chord reggae number called "Electric Avenue," that would, a few years later, resurface with slightly altered lyrics as an advertisement for Montgomery Ward. And every time I hear that commercial, I remember that dead girl, strangled in her upstairs apartment.

I guess I knew her, at the very least I had seen her, I knew her face. She was the type you always saw mousing around at the back of the club, a slight shy thing, someone's plain-faced friend. She wore glasses and no makeup, and somehow I had the impression she was a student at Centenary College in Shreveport.

I knew her boyfriend a bit better. He worked at the best bookstore in the city, and he always spoke to me when I came in. He wore his hair long like a graduate student, and sometimes he pulled it back tight in a ponytail. He favored faded chambray work shirts and round wire-rimmed glasses that made him look like a communist. These days I think of him as having a dark aspect, a hollowed-out and hungry look about him, but maybe that is only because I know what I know.

I know he was the suspect, the only one the police ever had. I know they thought he had snapped and murdered her. The detectives were never much concerned with why he might have done it; they approached the case methodically, and when he could not adequately account for his whereabouts that evening —he claimed he was home, reading and listening to music— they decided he must have been the one. There is no real science to it; it is usually the boyfriend or the husband or the father or the friend. Murder is an intimate crime. Statistics show that murderers usually know their victims well—they often love their victims. Love and jealousy and hate and rage—cops know it all gets mixed up and sometimes things go wrong and that sometimes "decent" people kill. The cops knew what Goethe knew; the way they figured it, given the right circumstances, the right pressures, everyone was capable of murder and worse.

It was a little complicated because not only did I know he was a suspect, I also knew he knew he was a suspect. He could not help but know it. After coming down to the detectives' office for a couple of interviews, he decided he needed an attorney and he did not talk to the cops again. He went to work and he went to class and sometimes you might see him buying a cup of frozen yogurt or flipping through the bins at a neighborhood record store.

He liked the blues; I remember watching him as he examined the jacket of Muddy Waters's *Hard Again,* peering at the list of songs and their running times. There was a black-and-white photo of Waters's roughened hands that suggested the luster of tarnished silver. I don't know whether he bought that album or not, whether he took it home and put it on his turntable and let the needle carve up the vinyl, whether he sat there in the dark with Muddy Waters groaning beautifully and thought about his murdered girlfriend.

A year passes, and then another. A grand jury is impaneled, but nothing comes of it. The boyfriend is called to testify, yet there is no evidence to speak of, just the conviction of certain police detectives.

They grumble, but after a while the case moves off the desk and into a steel file cabinet. The boyfriend manages to nod at faces he recognizes; he still goes to work and—after a decent interval—maybe he goes out to clubs again. Finally, he moves away. Sometimes things end this way; sometimes there is no denouement.

I don't know where he has gone.

Or why it is that I so often think about this particular case. It is, in so many ways, an ordinary murder, almost an accident. These things happen, wild blind things break the surface, then roll and disappear back into the black waters of the gut. I think he did it, too, but only because he always seemed so quiet and so sternly sad.

Because the police suspected him. Because I cannot imagine anyone else killing her.

And because I may be wrong, because my belief in his guilt is not based in anything the police ever told or showed me, I hope he never knew that I knew he was a suspect. I hope that I never betrayed my special journalistic knowledge. It seems unlikely that I did; I'm sure I was as vague a presence to him as he was to me in the days before he became a murder suspect. I'm not sure he knew my name or what I did for a living. I'm sure he couldn't have guessed that I drank stale coffee with the cops and that I had seen the inside of his girlfriend's apartment and photographs of her body with the bloody towel still wrapped around her neck.

He could not have known I had started a file with his name on it or that I anticipated his arrest. Or that I made notes on the books I saw him carrying and the music he played when he was working at the bookstore. Once I came into the bookstore and saw him leaning back in a chair behind the register, reading Giambattista Vico's *Scienza Nuova* while Robert Johnson's "Me and the Devil Blues" played on a small cassette machine:

> *Me and the devil was walkin' side by side*
> *Me and the devil, oooh, was walkin' side by side*
> *I'm gonna beat my woman, 'til I get satisfied . . .*

When Vico was a small boy, he fell headfirst off a ladder. For a while, it looked as though he might die. Though he didn't, in his autobiography he attributed the "melancholy nature" that afflicted his entire life to that early injury.

So Vico began to pick the world apart. His blues seem not so different from Robert Johnson's or the boyfriend's; we are all changed by the damage we sustain. Pain is what causes us to examine our lives—it is what makes us philosophers and poets. An eighteenth-century Italian does one thing; a black man from Mississippi does another.

And maybe boyfriends and reporters do something else again. But we all wake up in a painful world, where a radio commercial's electric guitar riff aches like something cold and black rising in our poor doomed lungs.

(1995)

Christmas in NYC

Her voice was full of money.

—F. Scott Fitzgerald,
The Great Gatsby

Fifth Avenue boils with human enterprise; the currents are strong. If you step out onto the sidewalk you run the risk of being pulled along with the others. At 4:30 P.M. the sky is darkening but everywhere candy lights hum red and gold. It's Christmastime in the city.

Shopping is what most of these people are engaged in; some look and some buy. Most buy; sooner or later we all buy. They've thrown up velvet ropes to channel the crowds past the gaudy window displays of Saks. A man in uniform stands at the store's entrance, regulating the flow of contestants into the arena.

America is a rich country, a country where most people have their basic needs met, a country that can support fashion. Even our poor are relatively well off, when compared with Guatemalan peasants or the beggars of Calcutta.

In America, even the homeless have shopping carts.

Americans shop for entertainment as well as to fulfill needs genuine and artificial. Some of us might find it natural that we get satisfaction and enjoyment from shopping; some even hold that the degree of pleasure one derives from a purchase is directly proportionate to the amount of money one spends. It seems we're buying not only the utility of the product, but a thrill—buying a packet of gum might elicit a tiny, barely noticeable shiver of delight, while buying a new car might jazz one's system for weeks.

Capitalism has created a world where the main striving for happiness comes not from hard and honest work but from the acquisition of things. Advertising generates wishes, and shopping temporarily slakes desire. More wishes, of course, quickly accrue, sticking in the consumer's heart. This is how our economy works, and whatever one may think of the morality of such a system, it works exceedingly well.

Such was not always the case; the role of the advertiser and the merchant have not always been so prominent. As late as the Civil War, the act of buying could hardly be thought of as recreational. Some folks hardly bought at all—they grew their own food, sewed their own clothes, and built their own shelter. They improvised and bartered and did without all manner of things we might today consider essential.

In his monumental 1993 book, *Land of Desire,* historian William Leach examines how, in the last years of the nineteenth century, this distinct culture of consumerism began to emerge— driven by a handful of merchant princes—people like John Wanamaker in Philadelphia, Marshall Field in Chicago, and the Straus brothers in New York. At the core of this culture was the drive for pleasure, comfort, and material acquisition.

"It speaks to us only of ourselves, our pleasures, our life," wrote the curiously skeptical merchant Herbert Duce in his 1912 book *Poster Advertising.* "It does not say, 'Pray, obey, sacrifice thyself, respect the King, fear thy master.' It whispers, 'Amuse thyself, take care of yourself.' Is this not the natural and logical effect of an age of individualism?"

Indeed, this new culture of consumerism was unconnected to—though not exactly opposed to—traditional notions of family and community values, to citizenship and religion. Absolutely secular, it based its moral sensibility on the central assumption that the exchange and circulation of money and goods was a positive force for society. It transformed America into a country where acquisition and consumption was seen by many as the foremost and perhaps the most important means of achieving happiness.

Buying stuff became a means of self-fulfillment, assuming the role of work and religion. This idea fit in neatly with the vision of America as a land of plenty, a kind of Eden Redux where all longings might be satisfied. Many Protestant settlers in the New World believed America would be where the millenial promise—the return of Jesus Christ—would occur and that His thousand-year reign would yield not only spiritual refreshment and salvation but streets literally paved with gold.

In the years before the First World War, as more and more Americans found themselves in positions to spend, more and more businesses dedicated to providing the individual with diversion and pleasure—restaurants, theaters, department stores—appeared. Commercialization transformed and vulgarized the American myth, separating it from any religious underpinning, and deeming the pursuit of goods as an acceptable avenue to "good."

"This world seems real only when it answers our individual touch," the early advertising mogul Artemus Ward wrote in 1892. "Yet, beyond our touch, beyond our waking, and almost in the land of dreams, lie things beyond our present thought, greater, wider, stronger than those which we now lay hold on. To each a world opens; to everyone possibilities are present."

Every child could grow up to be president, or better yet, a millionaire. Horatio Alger's Ragged Dick could rise from the streets to the board rooms, could become a captain of the earth. In the New World, peopled by consumers, people ready and able to buy and thus re-invent themselves as possessors, all things were possible. All men were free to dream, and—unconstricted by class—to realize those dreams. Wishes were available to all, and advertising men set out to create and implant them in the populace.

New Thought, Christian Science, and Unity emerged—new religious groups suited to the new culture. By and large these were optimistic, sunny worldviews that emphasized the importance of self-confidence and good cheer. This new theosophic view of the world broke into the popular culture in the early part of the twentieth century, in books like Eleanor Porter's *Pollyanna* and L. Frank Baum's *The Wonderful Wizard of Oz*.

In *Pollyanna*, the protagonist is a remarkably resilient eleven-year-old girl who never despairs or stops feeling "glad" despite a series of near biblical tribulations. Throughout the book her winning personality affects the drab and pitiful "sad" people she encounters; even after her legs are paralyzed in an automobile accident, she never gives up, never stops feeling "glad" about "rainbows" and "ice cream." (In the end, Pollyanna's buoyant optimism is rewarded by complete recovery—and she has transformed her town into a place where factory workers are "glad for Monday mornings.")

"People radiate what is in their minds and in their hearts," an instructive passage reads. "If a man feels kindly and obliging, his neighbors will feel the same way, too, before long. But if he scolds and growls and criticizes—his neighbors will scowl for scowl and add interest."

One of the most intriguing things about *Pollyanna* is the book's attitude toward the frugal; it characterizes savers as repressed Scrooges, unable to "enjoy life." Pollyanna loves stores and loves buying pretty things.

No wonder that *Pollyanna* was one of department store magnate John Wanamaker's favorite books, a work he pressed on friends, family, and employees.

"*Pollyanna* offered the same moral recipes as (French cleric Charles Wagner's book) *The Simple Life,*" Leach writes; "[D]on't think too much, enjoy life, be temperate and good, and always look on the bright side."

Leach recognized that Frank Baum's *The Wonderful Wizard of Oz* was even more successful at promulgating the fundamental tenets of the rising consumer culture.

Born in very comfortable circumstances, Baum rejected his father's world of oil fields and investment banking. Yet Baum was a true capitalist. He was simply drawn to the other side of it—the dreamy, fantastic, consumptive side.

"To gain all the meat from the nut of life is the essence of wisdom," Baum once told a newspaper reporter, "therefore 'eat, drink, and be merry'—for tomorrow you die."

Throughout his life, Baum followed his own advice; when he felt depressed he would treat himself to extravagant shopping sprees, often borrowing money to finance his therapy.

While Baum is famous for his Oz stories, it can be argued that his career as an expert on department store window dressing and display strategies was just as important to the development of American culture as his literary adventures—Baum all but invented window displays—and in 1898 he founded the National Association of Window Trimmers, an organization dedicated to "the uplifting of the mercantile decorating."

"It is said that people are not as readily deceived by a window display, but we all know better than this," Baum wrote in his 1900 book *The Art of Decorating Dry Goods Windows and Interiors.* He further believed that "without advertising, the modern merchant sinks into oblivion."

The Wonderful Wizard of Oz, first published in 1900, is perhaps one of the most significant American books—it certainly was one of the most popular. A sensation when it was new, it retains its currency today, a thoroughly American fairy tale that completely endorsed the coming American ethic of consumerism.

In Oz, there is nothing to feel guilty about, no drudgery, and very little conflict (remember that both evil witches are dispatched by accident—Dorothy doesn't mean to kill either one). Dorothy's journey is relatively painless, free of strict judgments and terror (Dorothy, good little Pollyanna that she is, is never frightened of anything for very long; even when she realizes the Wizard has tricked her, she quickly forgives the little man).

And Dorothy returns home—to dreary Kansas—via the "silver slippers" (changed to ruby slippers for the film). It's all a matter of attitude, of looking on the bright side. Things will work out.

Further on up the avenue, Trump Tower looms like a great spire of Oz. Most of the people who ride the escalators and flow through its halls aren't really interested in buying the gaudy baubles beyond the glass, the paintings, the silk ties, the leather purses, or the jewelry. They seem simply content to know that these items are there, waiting for them, over their particular rainbow.

(1995)

In Paris

I am looking out my window at the towers of Notre Dame on a clear cool morning and thinking about Rilke and Chekhov and the limits of desire.

Chekhov was clear about such things; he thought we were born to be disillusioned. We enter innocent but soon acquire knowledge. With knowledge, particularly the knowledge of our own mortality, comes fear. After we've reached this realization, after we've matured, we are doomed to experience only fragmentary happiness—with the old grump's definition of "happiness" grimly delineated as the temporary lifting of pain.

This morning the pain has lifted; beneath my window I hear the soft and excited burble of French vowels. Horsemen are clacking up the street, soldiers in dress uniform, their mounts sorted by colors. First come the chestnuts, then a narrow line of black, then dappled grays, then bays, then black again. Today is Armistice Day, a day that means much to the French—today they will allow their beribboned veterans to park their cars at crazy angles in the *Rue George V.*

I imagine the soldiers are on their way to the Arc de Triomphe, that loud monument to Napolean's hubris through which the Germans used to march every few years. Later we will follow the cavalry, make our own way up the *Champs-Elysee* and to the Arc itself.

But there will be time for tramping later; right now I have a few spare minutes, a chance to scratch down a few notes, a few impressions, something that I might run in the newspaper. And all I can come up with is how good it is to sit in my hotel window and look across two hundred yards of gray French air to Notre Dame while the woman I love showers and towels off after her morning run.

Bonjour, sweetheart—I am thinking of Chekhov, and I am thinking he was wrong.

•   •   •

Everyone has a history, and possibly regrets. Right now, I can't think of anything I would change, for any adjustment of the past might have set me on a trajectory that would have led me somewhere other than this room on this morning. Lots of people wind up worse off than content, though Chekhov would hold that only fools are truly happy.

There is something to that. Some people crave the company of the wildly neurotic and the damned; they think the straight life bland and sad. I understand the impulse to rip off one's clothes and to howl in the street, to flail against the indignities inflicted by living. Life is hard. It wears you out to face the petty and the mean, to look day after day into the blank uncomprehending eyes of your fellow animals.

I think I understand why desperate men nestle in trees with rifles, why someone might feel compelled to kill a Rabin or Lincoln or take the gas like Plath. I think I understand why awful things happen; there are some people whose wiring is a little different, who take certain things more or less to heart. We are all capable of doing things we would not like to become public knowledge, of hurling ourselves against the seemingly arbitrary gates of civilized life.

And maybe everyone needs to go through some of that, to wake up in strange rooms where neither your American accent nor your money does you good. I think maybe I've been through some of that myself, and maybe I am lucky to have come out the other side. You can get pulled apart in there, in that blistering maelstrom of desire.

I count myself lucky to have found a conspirator in sanity, someone who understands that what I need isn't always the same as what I want, and that wanting in itself can be a trap.

Life is too short to be a pain in the butt, she says, and no one wants to be around you if that's what you decide to be. What more do we need than the quiet pleasures—books and music and food and wine and the miracle of *Sainte-Chapelle*?

We are in love and in Paris, and you can think too much about Chekhov.

•   •   •

I am thinking about Rilke, too, or rather about something Rilke wrote to his "young poet" friend:

Works of art are of an infinite solitude, and no means of approach is so useless as criticism. Only love can touch them and hold them and be fair to them—Always trust yourself and your own feeling. . . . If it turns out you are wrong, then the natural growth of your inner life will eventually guide you to other insights. Allow your judgments their own silent, undisturbed development, which, like all progress, cannot be forced or hastened.

Rilke thought journalism an essentially dishonest enterprise, an attack on the existence of art. And, as anyone who works for a newspaper would, I wonder about that sometimes—especially since I find myself in accord with most of Rilke's thought. Even as a practicing critic, I believe in his warnings against criticism—it is, at times, destructive to seeing things fresh.

And I believe it is important to try to see things fresh, to allow for the sneaky joy of little moments.

Chekhov, for all his wonder powers of summation and distillation, could never see things fresh—he was constitutionally opposed to wonder. At the end, there always comes the moment of disillusionment. What was desired turns poison in the mouth. Love fades, the tingles dim, the father dies, the solemn blanket of certainty ineluctably descends. Game over. Fin.

Chekhov could have written for the newspaper. He might have made a damn good city editor.

But what is factual and inevitable is not always what is true; what is true is what hops in your breast, what fills your lungs. There are things that are ineffable and that cannot be explained, things that make your skin crawl and sear your heart—things that might make the statues cry.

I am looking out across the Seine, above the oldest street in Paris, while a parade clacks along beneath my feet, separated from my love by an inch-thick bathroom door, on Armistice Day, and, as near as I can tell, I am supremely, impossibly, completely happy.

(1995)

Click Song: Some Blues for Dr. King

Some night soon, white boy, you get into your fancy car and drive. You drive hard and solo, maybe with the window cracked, an icy whistle threading past your ear, the radio lamp glowing cool undersea green. Mindless, you drive deep, with city lights receding to a vague half-halo, a gray shimmering over black pines. You drive, into the purple velvet flatness of the Delta with Jimmy Reed moaning, his voice spiked with mad pain. Something in his vibrato makes your chest contract, your heart ripen. Thump it, and it might burst, so full of tears and blood it seems.

Headlights grope for an oatmeal highway, then slide onto a gravel shoulder and die in the balding grass lot of a tonk held together by rusted tin signs and dry paint-less boards. Your leather shoes crunch on the frozen dirt, slip a bit on the joint's smooth-worn steps. You fall inside, awkward as a skating drunk, and the screen door bangs behind you.

At first you can't see but feel the warm, oily air, burnished gold by gas heaters and an old wood stove. Cotton and chocolate swim at you through convection waves; a few old heads turn toward you, smile mild smiles, then turn back to their beers, their game of dominoes, whatever held their interest before you came in. A jukebox plays Clarence Carter, one of those nasty double entendre songs, and an old woman, a nylon scarf pulled over plastic curlers, dances by herself.

You get a drink from a wizened man behind the bar. Whiskey burns a tangled string in your gullet, spreading warm through your body like swallowed plutonium. A younger man is shooting pool alone. He keeps his head cocked down, one eye sighted down the cue like a sniper; he means to strike it true.

Put your quarters down on the table, white boy; maybe you want to play him, make him your friend. He nods at you, a level look—you pick a stick out of the rack and are surprised at its lack of heft; in the rough places they take the lead weights out of the butt end of the cue. They swing like kindling that way and are less useful in a fight. Your would-be friend takes your quarters and slips them in the metal template, jams it in, and the balls drop out, each with its own discrete thwock, like lazy raindrops. With a few easy turns of legerdemain—the balls fit like marbles in his big hands—he presumes to rack them and offers you the break.

Yet there is no power in your light stick. The white ball bounces off the rack, almost effectless, and for the first time he curls his mouth into a grin. He takes the loosened seven ball hard into the right corner pocket, spinning the cue ball off the rail and into the back of the rack, scattering the field. Something drops into some pocket as an afterthought.

You are surely outclassed. You watch him pick off another solid ball, then another, then another. He misses when the five ball rattles against the plastic sleeve in the side pocket and pops out. Too hard, he mutters.

You shoot and miss, and he finishes his run. He taps a pocket with his cue and banks the eight ball into it. You lose.

• • •

You want to know humility, white boy, you go to where the humble people go. This ain't anthropology, this is still America.

Maybe you got a bookcase tight with the black intellectuals, from W. E. B. DuBois and Oliver Cromwell Cox to Cornel West, from Stanley Crouch to Greg Tate and Derrick Bell. Maybe there's a fresh copy of Michael Eric Dyson's *Making Malcolm: The Myth and Meaning of Malcolm X* sitting on your desk at home.

Maybe you've written about Huddie Ledbetter, done enough research on the man considered to be the confluence of white folk music and black blues to understand he didn't appreciate being called "Leadbelly." Maybe you have developed a private theory of black aesthetics, listened to a lot of rap music, and even played rhythm guitar in a lousy blues band.

You still ain't black, Jack.

• • •

And it's funny that part of you wants to be; that just like Mr. Mailer said, there is present in you a tender longing for the conferred hipness of blackness. You want that outlaw gene that Hollywood conjured, to be damaged and dangerous; you want the alarming militant cool of a fierce brother. You Artificial Negro, you poseur, you sorry patronizing white boy, come with open wallet to purchase some street credibility.

It is ironic that even as young black men are murdered, maimed, and imprisoned in record numbers, their style has become disproportionately influential in shaping American popular culture. Blacks are athletes and entertainers, gangsters and scapegoats. For all the talk of equality of opportunity and blithering about something called multiculturalism, blacks remain—nearly thirty years after the murder of the Reverend Dr. Martin Luther King—if not a genuine underclass, at least an under-caste —for in today's America only whiteness admits you to full and unconditional citizenship.

And people wonder why the most prominent black political voice in the country belongs to a black nationalist, a former calypso singer named Louis Farrakhan. Maybe we ought not wonder why the man who most convincingly articulates the black conscience isn't a conciliator, but a separatist who urges blacks to free themselves from "the enemy"—the white establishment— and preaches self-sufficiency.

• • •

You say you can't understand hate—and Farrakhan does hate—but maybe you can understand that there comes a time to stop relying on the promises of a nation that has broken your heart and martyred your saints. Dreams are still deferred, and the empire is striking back, preparing to make war on the poor (who, after all, would not be poor if they could only learn some self-discipline and for God's sake turn down those awful boom boxes).

Go ahead, white boy, rant on about your tough love approach to welfare and the need to move unruly young black men out of school and into prison. Listen to Aretha Franklin to prove you're not a racist.

And thank God there was a Martin Luther King Jr. and that so many Americans still follow his example.

(1995)

Forgiving Elvis

Jim lives in Chicago—Clark and Division—and he has never been to Memphis. So on a Saturday morning a few of us load a cooler in the car and head east, our itinerary written in the windwash of tractor-trailer rigs. Like Muslims to Mecca, we are drawn to Graceland.

Our trip is essentially a goof, a chance to buy a ticket and prowl around the sanctified grounds where, sixteen years on, what some might call glum-struck white trash stare balefully at Elvis Presley's grave. Maybe we go to Graceland hoping to recover something half-forgotten and dear, or to hack away at the gnarled pathology of the terrified Boy King, but while we're there we get our kicks from *schadenfreude.*

So, it is really an ugly and unkind impulse—the thrill of voyeurism—that carries us through those famous gates up to the smaller-than-expected house with its baffling mirrors, fifteen-foot white sofa and fourteen RCA television sets. But while Graceland allows us to snigger at lush kitsch it also forces us to contemplate a brand of innocence unavailable to twenty-one-year-old truck drivers today.

Those who've written about Elvis Presley have often seized on the words of William Carlos Williams: "The pure products of America go crazy." Tramp through this garish monument, this Pharoah's tomb, and understand that as Elvis grew deeply crazy he remained utterly pure. His taste for banal comforts, his pool table, his "Jungle Room" with its carpeted ceiling is touching and heart-cracking, in its way as wretchedly and wonderfully Southern as the crudely pious paintings of Howard Finster or the grotesque fables of cracker writer Harry Crews.

Of course Graceland is filigreed in the breathless, impatient style of one who has risen fast and who knows he may fall hard. Elvis, bloated and dead at forty-two, never quite believed in his own success. He squandered his talent in indifferent recordings and silly movies; he wanted to be Bing Crosby while we wanted him to be James Dean—forever young and smoldering with animal ardor. Maybe Elvis wasn't too smart (and then again, maybe he was) but maybe he was smart enough to know what he wasn't, maybe we drove him inside these gates and into this lurid, yellow-leathered den with Red and Sonny.

There is a telling, chilling moment on the Graceland tour. In what was Daddy Vernon's office, they play a snippet of video for the tourists; in it, young Elvis, just back from his army tour in Germany, pledges to hold onto Graceland "for just as long as [he] can."

It is Graceland that has held on to poor deathless Elvis. Here he has been Disneyfied and de-sexed, molded into something creamy and porcelain-cool, as bland and hollow as one of Jeff Koon's ceramic icons. In the meditation garden, the inattention and camp continue; Elvis's middle name "Aron" is misspelled "Aaron" on his memorial plaque and Vernon's marker bears a copyright notice.

Still, there is an undeniable *frisson* that comes with such proximity to Elvis Presley. It is as if Graceland has atomized him; his funk gets in your clothes and your hair and follows you to bed hundreds of miles away.

In the inevitable gift shop, Jim buys souvenirs. He chooses an extravagant pair of sunglasses, some Elvis antiperspirant and—at my suggestion—a compact disc of the *Sun Sessions*. These are Elvis's earliest recordings, made in Memphis with Sam Phillips, and they still represent his best work—scary genius stuff. Though the Graceland guides assure us it was a good thing that Elvis moved from the small Sun label to the giant RCA, these are the important sounds—just Elvis and Scotty Moore and Bill Black fooling around in the studio.

Later we sit in a darkened house and listen to that keening tenor—not so dark or mannered as it became in later years— and expunge our grief. And ask Elvis's forgiveness.

(1993)

Assassination Thing

Assassination—the murder of a captain of the earth—does not require a high conspiracy. Anyone could do it, alone.

Francisco Martin Duran, the young man accused of spraying the White House with bullets, may or may not have been trying to kill the president. He might have assumed he would be cut down by Secret Service snipers before he could maneuver his Chinese-made semi-automatic weapon into position to fire; he might have imagined a clever path to suicide.

That's what they said about the semi-skilled pilot who crashed a stolen Cessna on the White House lawn, that he probably wasn't trying to kill anyone but himself. That's what they say, and you can believe it if you want to.

Yet it is important to remember that no confederacy of mobsters and government operatives is necessary to kill a big man. All it takes is wretched patience and will, a fistful of cash, and a cheap pistol. Sooner or later the parade will pass.

Still, it is more than annoying to think that a dirty-necked pipsqueak with bulging eyes could—in six dingy seconds—insinuate himself into our national consciousness. It offends the natural order of things; it doesn't suit our sense of Homeric drama. We prefer to invent conspiracies, to believe in spindly webs of intrigue, an invisible network of actual power. So some of us believe the Czar's *Okhrana* set up Bogrov to murder the reformer Stolypin in Kiev in 1911. So some imagine Lincoln's tomb empty, and that the great man died anonymous in bed, and that John Wilkes Boothe was played for a patsy by Edward Stanton. We are greedy for nonsense, for the great unlocking secrets.

But Lee Harvey Oswald killed John F. Kennedy. No one can change that, not Oliver Stone with his mad and beautiful dreams, not that lawyer down in Texas who says that LBJ arranged the whole thing. Though we cannot prove the sniper acted alone, without the complicity of others, there is no compelling reason to believe any of the filigreed theories. Take Ockham's Razor to the tangle of circumstance and coincidence and a simple, if unsatisfying, answer presents itself.

Kennedy was a complex man of contradictory appetites; he made many enemies. Some people need to affirm their existence by destruction. They only know they are real when they are taking something down. Men kill for banal reasons, to boost their self-esteem and to change the world. You and I have known our Oswalds, swampy-headed folks with bits of uncongealed philosophy sloshing around in their heads. We have noticed them in the hard, narrow carrels of libraries, digging and scribbling their way through heavy books by skimpy theorists. They stalk the genuine villains of the age with yellowed clippings in their pockets and grim phobias in their hearts. We have all met these shy insurrectionists, and we have dismissed them as sad and ineffectual. It helps us to sleep.

Most of the time their plots get no further than the bed-sitter apartments they invariably inhabit. Only sometimes they break through and flash—hot and brief as comets—across the headlines. What is surprising is that more of them don't wander stunned and leaking down Pennsylvania Avenue, looking for the kill.

What was it that H. Rap Brown used to say—that violence is as American as cherry pie? Better to realize that there is nothing particularly American about it. Maybe Americans are good at turning violence into something to be consumed, but violence attaches to the dominion of man when we brutalize each other.

●　　●　　●

It is almost always one person, one gun.

On July 2, 1881, a deluded religious zealot named Charles Guiteau tiptoed out of the men's room of a Washington train station and fired two shots into the back of President James A. Garfield, killing him. Guiteau—who, by the way, called himself a "crank," thus popularizing the use of the word to describe a deranged person—was hanged before a crowd of four thousand the next year. On the gallows, he squinced his voice into falsetto and sang "I am going to the Lordy, I am so glad."

Nearly a year into his second term, President William

McKinley was greeting visitors in a reception line at the Pan-American Exposition in Buffalo when he was shot twice by the anarchist Czolgosz, who had secreted a derringer in his bandaged hand. Eight days later the president was dead.

Theodore Roosevelt was more fortunate. Three weeks before the presidential election of 1912, John Schrank, a Milwaukee saloonkeeper, shot the Progressive party candidate while Roosevelt was on his way to deliver a major campaign speech. In one of the more remarkable gestures of political bravado of this or any other century, Roosevelt refused to go to the hospital, insisting he would "give this speech or die." He arrived at the hall and spoke for fifty minutes, referring to his would-be assassin as "that poor creature" before leaving to seek medical attention.

Later, an examination revealed that Schrank's bullet had struck both Roosevelt's steel pince-nez case and a folded copy of his speech, apparently slowing the slug enough to save his life. Schrank, later declared insane by a court, announced he was motivated by a deep hatred of Roosevelt that had its roots in TR's desire for a third term.

In 1933, the madman Zangara fired at President-elect Franklin Delano Roosevelt and killed Chicago mayor Cermak during an appearance in Miami's Bayfront Park. Even the benign-seeming Gerald Ford was targeted by loners with guns. In September 1975, he survived two separate attempts on his life. Squeaky Fromme tried to shoot at him in Sacramento, but her .45 caliber pistol jammed. Eighteen days later, in San Francisco, Sara Jane Moore got to within thirty-five feet of the president and fired a shot. An alert ex-marine deflected her aim. Ronald Reagan was our second president shot on television; he survived Hinckley's bullets but another presidential assassination was closer than we knew at the time.

Now two attempts—maybe—on Bill Clinton. In this age of hate and political polarization, can we be surprised? Anyone who believes violence is something un-American, something outside our ken, is demonstrably and remarkably naive. Violence is an ignoble catalyst, perhaps, but it has played its role in every phase of the American struggle. We ought to understand that and know that some of the people who hate this president or any other might be capable of converting their vicious rhetoric into vicious action.

On the evening of November 22, 1963, broadcast newsman Edwin Newman, looking not significantly younger than he does today, stared into an NBC camera and told a pulverized nation what it needed to hear.

"This event is unreal," he said, "absurd—one of the things that we just don't let happen. But if one in 190 million wants to kill the President, he will."

He will. He can. It hasn't happened in more than three decades, but our country—our world—has no shortage of little men capable of acting alone, of sighting down the scope of a mail-order Mannlicher-Carcano, catching a famous head in the cross hairs, and squeezing into the history books.

(1994)

Blood Requites

On a Friday in Hebron—on the first day of the festival of Purim when Jews commemorate the hanging of Haman, an officer of the Persian king Ahasuerus who had plotted to destroy the Jews—a thirty-eight-year-old doctor from Brooklyn dressed in a soldier's uniform walked into the Cave of the Patriarchs where Abraham is buried and leveled a Galil assault rifle at the crowd of praying Palestinians.

Benjy Goldstein squeezed and held his trigger until the thirty-five-round clip was empty. He then inserted another clip and sprayed again. Another clip. And then another.

Some of the survivors claim he also tossed three hand grenades into the crowd; some say there were other gunmen.

Finally, desperate Palestinians overcame Goldstein and beat him to death with iron bars and a fire extinguisher. Had they not finally charged him, he would have killed more than the forty or so he did on that first day of Purim—the day the Jews fight back.

"On that day the Jews united . . . to fall on all those who had planned their ruin," the Book of Esther recounts. "So that the Jews put their enemies to the sword, with great slaughter and destruction; they worked their will on those who hated them."

Benjy Goldstein, it is supposed, had been profoundly affected by the assassination of the radical rabbi Meir Kahane in New York City in 1990. His friends say he often talked about killing Arabs. While he might seem to fit into the classic "mad loner" construct, Goldstein was also the product of a paranoid subculture that has often been subjected to atrocity and has often responded with desperate violence.

Hebron is a seat of radicalism. It was the place where, in 1929, Arabs killed sixty-seven Jews. Seven years later, the Jews in Hebron were attacked again—and evacuated. They returned after the 1967 war, with the first settlers squatting in a local hotel. Since then, Hebron has become a place for the most fevered and seething elements of Zionism. Young radicalized

Jews from Brooklyn—followers of the hypermilitant Kahane, members of the Jewish Defense League and Kach—have taken up residency there, in the lap of their Palestinian "enemies."

•   •   •

Fanaticism demands "enemies." To be entitled to revenge, one needs an oppressor to strike out at. Benjy Goldstein—the avenger of the Jews—found his "oppressors" kneeling in prayer. Michael F. Griffin—the avenger of inchoate souls—found his outside a Florida abortion clinic.

One can imagine Benjy Goldstein dying in a kind of ecstasy, believing that his murderous impulses were justified. To some he is a hero, for he may have seriously damaged the prospects for the mutual accommodation of Arabs and Jews in the Middle East.

Michael Griffin too must endure admirers and apologists, though he was not fortunate enough to have been killed on the spot by pro-choice advocates. But while the defense mounted by Griffin's lawyers—they claimed their client was not culpable because he was in the thrall of a lay minister leading a nonviolent antiabortion march at the time of the shooting—is legally ludicrous, there are indeed moral consequences to protected speech.

In this country we are allowed to say whatever we want, whether we believe it or not, with few restrictions. It is not against the law to preach that the Holocaust never happened or that black folk are an inferior tribe of mud people. Khalid Muhammad is not a criminal; neither is Rush Limbaugh.

One of the more troubling aspects of this country's so-called "culture war" between an amoral left and a "Christian right" is the willingness of those who imagine themselves on one side or the other of the argument to appropriate a grammar of victimization. It is especially distressing to hear Christians whining about their supposed disconnection from the political mainstream when, in fact, the Christian tradition is the dominate theme of the national fugue.

Those who imagine themselves persecuted in a land where they control so much are flirting with the kind of madness that finds in religion excuses to act on their fear of others. In such an atmosphere, it is reasonable to expect that some marginal individuals like Benjy Goldstein and Michael Griffin, fed by the overwrought rhetoric of the long-denied, will commit to jihad.

A few days after Goldstein's slaughter, a man named Rashad Baz was arrested for attempted murder after he allegedly shot four Jewish Hasidim in a van. Baz told the police the van's driver had tried to cut him off near an approach to the Brooklyn Bridge; a buddy arrested along with Baz said his friend was enraged by the Hebron massacre. Violence inevitably spirals when only blood requites blood.

(1994)

God and Man
in the Land of Mod

A reporter for a local business journal that takes an interest in reporting on the media, a woman named Dixie Walters, called to say she was preparing a story about the role of religion in the lives of people who comment on the news. She used the rather elegant term "opinion journalists."

I have seen her story and have no complaints. She did a fine job of reporting what I said, and I suspect she did as well with the others she interviewed. Though journalists are notoriously tough interviews—perhaps even more than regular folks we are suspicious of the note taker at the other end of the phone; we know too well the traps that may be set and how the prey can be exposed in print—she managed to cobble together an interesting survey. Seventeen commentators submitted to her questions; only two had the sense (and tamed egos) to decline her invitation to comment.

What emerged was a snapshot of the rather shaky belief system of what the snide might call an elite. It seems we "opinion journalists" are, as a group, probably about as "religious" as the population as a whole. Some of us go to church, most of us do not, yet only a few of us are brave (or, if you will, vapid) enough to dismiss the possibility of a higher intelligence.

(The only surprise was that I turned up somewhat right of center on the piety index, a fact that will no doubt interest some of my anonymous correspondents who have, on several occasions, assured me that the God of Love is not about to forgive my particular vanities and trespasses and is, in fact, concocting an especially strenuous afterlife for those of "my ilk.")

In any event, it ought to be soothing to some readers that most of us who write about issues of public concern—we "opinion journalists"—have at least a nodding acquaintance with the basic tenets of Judeo-Christian thought. But then, how could we not? Leaving aside the whining of a few self-styled victims,

American culture is shot through with religion; it informs every aspect of our daily lives.

Religion furnishes our inner life, whether or not we believe in angels; it's in our literature, in our music—from Bach's B Minor Mass to the forsaken chill of Robert Johnson to, yes, even the serious silliness of Madonna's pop sideshows. God—acknowledged or not, dead or not, creator of man or man's creation—abides.

• • •

Understand, there is a counterbalancing theme in our national fugue. America is a child of the Enlightenment, the first modern country. We have known no kings, we were the first colonial state to take that long step away from government by divine revelation and the absolute power of church and state. We were born in the Age of Reason, where rationalism and empirical methods have supplanted superstition and faith as the predominant ways of seeking to understand the world. America requires of its citizens a certain hard-won skepticism; our experience has taught us to be distrustful of power and those who seek it. We believe we ought to be wary of anyone who claims a tight connection with a higher power, especially if that someone proffers the keys to the kingdom of heaven in exchange for something as prosaic as money or political fealty.

I do not mean to pick on any of my colleagues who answered the survey, especially since what Ms. Walters wrote was necessarily brief and all quotes—no matter how carefully cleaned and lifted—are out of context. It would be easy to pick out a quote from one "opinion journalist" or another and rail against it. But, as St. Thomas Aquinas—and Richard Nixon—said, that would be wrong.

There was, however, a quote in the story that should not be allowed to pass without some observation.

"Reason is my guiding light," one of the columnists was quoted as saying. At first blush that might seem a statement of unconvincing bravado, or that of a lonely superman surveying a cold planet. Maybe it simply sounds like one of those things one simply says; it might induce giggles, or—in another context—inspire a kind of manly admiration for the speaker.

We Americans are a race of cynics, a people suspicious.

Maybe this is not such a bad thing; there are plenty of things to suspect and much that needs further investigation. But it seems to me that dry reason—Voltaire's greatest hit—is a lean, barely sufficient epistemology for reaching moral decisions.

Reason, unchecked by a compassionate humanism or religious teaching, invariably leads to the blind pursuit of self-interest. With nothing to answer to aside from our own appetites, with nothing to dissuade us from "immoral" actions aside from the risk assessment of the threat of punishment, we are nothing more than conniving monsters, nasty and blank inside. "Right" and "wrong" become nothing more than assessments of relative risk. It is wrong to do something that may enrich you if the level of risk is unacceptably high. Rightness depends entirely on one's self-confidence, suckers ought never be given an even break, any system exists to be exploited to the cusp of diminishing returns. That's where reason leads us.

We encounter these people—these rational beasts—regularly; we have a name for them, we call them sociopaths. They don't all wind up in prison. We find them in Congress, in business, in the desks beside us. They are the advantage takers, the margin pushers, the admirers of "gutsy" wheeler-dealers and the cool-hand hustlers.

"When one asks how a sense of guilt arises in anyone," Freud says in *Civilization and Its Discontents,* "one is told something one cannot dispute: people feel guilty—pious people call it 'sinful'—when they have done something they know to be 'bad.' But then one sees how little this answer tells one."

The desuetude of sin, as a concept, as an affront to the unspoken (and, as the old theologians used to say, *et in pluribus*—apparent to all) compact between men, is the most troubling aspect of life in modern America. And one need not be particularly pious to see it. Sin exists, as surely as Grace.

"All you need is love," the hippies sang, and that is not quite right. But we cannot do without it.

No one ought ever be required to believe in anything. Yet it seems to me that the night is dark and vast and our minds give off but puny light.

(1994)

Waiting for the End of the World

*"Dear Lord, I sincerely hope you're coming,
'cause you really started something."*

—Elvis Costello

All over America, a growing number of Bible-believing evangelicals have expressed an interest in apocalyptic prophecy, and the *fin de siècle* seems a natural hook on which to hang the cataclysmic end to the present age. While Americans have seemed to have an especial fondness for apocalyptic lore since William Miller's followers gathered in the fields to await the return of Christ in the mid-nineteenth century, current events and the approach of the year 2000 have again heightened interest in the End Times.

The twentieth century is almost over—surely the rolling over of the celestial odometer must mean something. This end-of-the-world thing seems like it may be pretty important stuff; we're told it's going to affect every one of us and so maybe we ought to pay attention to it. After all, there are those who believe that as sure as the Lord created the universe in six twenty-four-hour days, he's about ready to wrap the whole thing up. Saddam Hussein's mischief in the Persian Gulf is seen by some as the prelude to, if not—as Saddam himself has called it—"the mother of all battles."

The prophetic eschatology of some fundamentalist Christians holds that the countdown to Armageddon began with the formal establishment of the State of Israel in 1948, and that the miraculous six-day war in 1967, which put Israel in control of the Holy City of Jerusalem, was a necessary fulfillment of biblical prophecy.

Marilyn Hickey, a Denver-based evangelist with an extensive product catalogue (for $14.95 one can learn how to either *Satan*

Proof Your Home or *Stomp the Devil*), delivered five sessions of "study and multimedia presentation" and a line-by-line exegesis of the Book of Revelation at the nondenominational Agape Church in Little Rock last week. She believes we are "obviously in the end times" and that the year 2001 may bring the Second Coming of Christ and the dawning of the millennium: a thousand years of Christ's blissful rule on earth in which the "Overcomers"—those who have avoided being cast into the Lake of Fire—prepare and cleanse the world so that it might make a fit offering to God.

Framed by a pale peach marble proscenium, Hickey, a trim cheery woman of indeterminate age, addressed crowds of perhaps five hundred or more during her three-hour sessions. Christians (and possibly even some non-Christians) of all persuasions came to hear her, and during the final session there was heard hardly a murmur of dissent and much scratching of pens in checkbooks. Hickey believes everything in the Bible should "be taken as literally as you can take it," that the streets of the millennium capital New Jerusalem—which will be about half the size of the United States and hover over the old city of Jerusalem—*will* be made of gold, that the gates to the city *will* be of pearl.

(Why pearl of all the gemstones in the world? Because, Hickey explained, the Bible says so. And possibly because pearl is a "lively stone"—the only stone made by a living creature. And because in the parable about the "pearl of great price," Hickey understands the "pearl" to be symbolic of the souls of the faithful, which Christ gave up his life to recover. All in all, a fairly elegant argument.)

While Hickey's message is ultimately upbeat—at least for those confident in Jesus' glowing presence in their breast—it looks like a hard rain's a gonna fall before Christ comes again in glory to judge the quick and the dead.

Perhaps the trigger to all this, what we can start looking for any day now, is "the Rapture"—an event a Baptist minister named Edgar Whisenant kept setting dates for a few years ago. Though the term never appears in the Bible, it refers to a scene described in I Thessalonians 4:16, 17: "For the Lord Himself shall descend from heaven with a shout, with the voice of the archangel, and with the trumpet of God. And the dead in Christ shall rise first; then we who are alive and remain shall be caught up together with them in the clouds to meet the Lord in the air."

After the Rapture, after the more pious among us are transported to Heaven, a seven-year period of Tribulation will befall those left behind on earth, beginning with the appearance of a False Messiah—the Antichrist—as the leader of a ten-nation confederation. This False Messiah will appear to be a man of peace—and, Hickey averred, "very physically attractive." Hickey shares with many other fundamentalists the opinion that the Antichrist is already living here on earth, but refuses to join in the speculation as to his or her identity. In earlier times, Nero, Napoleon, Hitler, and even Johnny Rotten (who, after all, did claim the title) have been suspected. In the 1970s, many thought the globe-trotting Henry Kissinger might be the Antichrist.

One radio evangelist, David Webber, went so far as to note that in a numerological system in which the letter "A" was assigned the value six (the number of man, who was created on the sixth day), "B" assigned a value of 12, "C" a value of 18, and so forth, the numerical sum of "Kissinger" is 666—which, according to Revelation 13:16–18, is the designated "Mark of the Beast." Other potential Antichrists have included Anwar Sadat (who, when he reopened the Suez Canal to commercial navigation in 1975, was rumored to have ridden in a ship with 666 emblazoned on its side), Mikhail Gorbachev, and even Ronald Wilson Reagan. Notice how our ex-president, a former movie star who some credit more than Gorbachev with the break-up of the Soviet empire, has six letters in each of his three names.

Regardless of who it is—and not even Hal Lindsey, the best-selling apocalyptic author of *The Late Great Planet Earth* and other prophecy books, will take a stab at that one, other than to say the Antichrist is a "passionate humanist" who now lives somewhere in Europe—the Tribulation will be a tough time for all concerned. The Antichrist will seek power over all humanity by requiring that every person wear a mark or number (probably 666) in order to buy or sell. Those who refuse this mark will either starve or be slain; those who do accept it will be forever damned.

Hickey's Overcomers, of course, will be spared this choice, since they will have already been raptured up. On the other hand, some apocalyptics believe the Rapture will not come until well after the Tribulation starts, and that Christians should move to rural areas and lay in supplies in order to avoid the damnable mark.

At some point in the Tribulation, the Antichrist will be joined by the False Prophet, a religious leader who is often assumed in prophetic circles to be the Pope. As the world becomes increasingly corroded, the "army of the East" will gather in the plain of Megiddo and prepare to storm the Holy City. As the preparations for battle begin, Christ will return to the earth, descending on the Mount of Olive and watched by every human eye (quite possibly, Hickey says, through the satellite technology of CNN).

Christ will join the battle of Armageddon, and his armies—which may be made up of the Overcomers as well as the few faithful who have survived the Tribulation—will eventually overcome the Antichrist and the False Prophet, who will be slain and cast into a lake of fire. Satan, by the way, will be tied up in a bottomless pit, where he'll serve out the duration of the millennium. At the end of the thousand years of good feeling, Satan will be given one final chance to win some souls, and he will launch one final battle. At this point, God will stop kidding around and destroy the heretics by fire. Their souls will join the Antichrist and the False Prophet in the lake of fire, where they will be tormented forever. The earth itself will then be consumed by fire, and a new Heaven and a new earth will take its place. The Overcomers and the redeemed will live forever in bliss. Amen.

So there are some—those who believe Marilyn Hickey, for instance—who can take comfort that the end is apparently nigh. For them, it signals that the world will soon experience ecstasy, and that all our trials, Lord, soon will be over.

In the meantime, it might not be such a bad idea to Satan-proof our homes. My check is in the mail.

(1991)

Why Not Revenge?

America is still a fresh nation, more interested in doing and becoming than considering, so it is probably appropriate that Americans are more intuitive than intellectual. There is something raw and natural in us that resists overcivilization. Democracies are always prone to irrational decisions. Americans are the new barbarians; we are the ones who will yet change the world. Perhaps that is why we bray for blood.

There are no rational arguments for capital punishment that withstand scrutiny. It is no sure deterrent, it creates more problems than it solves. It is irreversible, and our courtrooms are imperfect. Yet eight out of ten of us want to retain it and the cathartic spasm that seems to be its only benefit.

Arguments pro and con have become boilerplate, but history provides us with some important evidence. First of all, the framers of the Constitution not only entertained the idea of capital punishment, they endorsed it. Second, in order to be constitutional, the death penalty must be applied consistently and rationally. Despite the safeguards invented by society, executions in America have not met this critical standard.

For most of his twenty-five years on the Supreme Court, Justice Harry A. Blackmun supported the death penalty. A week or so ago, he came to the conclusion that he could no longer support it. He announced his decision in a dissent on the Supreme Court's refusal to hear the appeal of a Texan scheduled to die by lethal injection for killing a bar patron during a holdup.

Blackmun's dissent begins with a melodramatic description of the expected execution.

That was, as we say in the biz, a weak lead. It provoked the usual, and undeniable, rebuttal from Justice Antonin Scalia. Those who die on gurneys in prison death chambers generally have it a lot better than their victims. Still, fine writing aside, Blackmun's case is concise and solid: if capital punishment is to be consistent, it ought be levied against everyone convicted of similar crimes. This is impossible, however, because the court requires that each defendant be treated as an individual, and that mitigating circumstances be considered. These two contradictory requirements, Blackmun claims, nullify the state's right to kill.

Of course, the majority of the court remains unconvinced by Blackmun's reasoning. Scalia's opinion even seems to suggest that one of the reasons for maintaining the death penalty is because an overwhelming majority of the American people favor it. Scalia, to be fair, mentions this only in passing, but such rhetoric is frustrating.

One of the costs of democracy is the stray irrational policy, the sop to the yahoo class, and the meaningless, feel-good proclamation. The Supreme Court exists, in part, to check the will of the majority. What has been most distressing about the Rehnquist court has been its tendency to majoritarianism.

Blackmun's decision was almost assuredly an act of conscience, if not an act of heroism. While cynics might consider it a signal of exasperation, or as the softening of an old man's head, Blackmun is right, in both his pragmatic approach and his ultimate decision.

Though the emotional, moral arguments against executions are perhaps the most compelling ones, the law requires a cooler approach. By focusing on the profound inequalities evident in the justice system, Blackmun has constructed a proof of almost mathematical integrity. No matter how popular the killing labs, so long as factors such as race, geography, class of victim, and socioeconomic status can be shown to bear on a defendant's likelihood of execution, the death penalty is an impermissible sanction.

●　　●　　●

Accept, for the moment, that capital punishment is not a deterrent to murder. (It probably is a deterrent to a lot of other crimes, but since we don't kill people for stealing cars or breaking windows, the question is irrelevant.) Accept that it doesn't do anything to restore the victim or the victim's family. Accept that it is monstrous to argue that killing is more cost-effective than warehousing a dangerous person for the rest of his or her natural life.

Accept all that, because it is true. Or accept all that because you can't know that it's not true. Most "civilized" nations have come to those conclusions and abolished capital punishment. But even if you don't buy those arguments, please bear with me—those issues are really tangential to this discussion—there are ways to answer those questions without joining this moral adventure. Accept the proffered premise: An execution is primarily an act of vengeance.

So, if the chief purpose of capital punishment is retaliation against a law-breaking individual, should we continue the practice? In other words, why not revenge?

It is a startling, assumption-challenging question. Invariably, the asker is angry and perhaps disingenuous: he thinks the state has not only the right but the duty to put to death those who violate its laws. It is possible he is more interested in rationalizing his emotional response to a vile crime than making a serious inquiry. Yet, even flippantly asked, it is a good question, one that deserves an answer. It requires the knee-jerk opponent of capital punishment to consider the position of those followers of Jesus—whose dying words were "Father, forgive them"—who nevertheless believe that murderers should die at the hands of the state.

More than 71 percent of all Americans believe that capital punishment is necessary and right. The percentage is slightly higher among those who call themselves Christians. One cannot assume that these millions are all callused people, honking for blood. Most of them are good folks, people capable of kindness and generosity of spirit.

There is plenty of biblical support for capital punishment, plenty of passages that mandate if a man does this or that he shall be put to death. And over the centuries, criminals have been more or less routinely killed by lawful authorities, often in the name of God. While the crimes that merit execution might change, only relatively recently has God's putative blessing on retributive capital punishment been seriously challenged.

Believers can point to any number of biblical passages supporting the notion of execution. The Mishnah, the first document of rabbinic Judaism, lists both capital crimes and acceptable modes of carrying out punishment. "Blood defiles the land, and expiation cannot be made on behalf of the land for blood shed on it except by the blood of the man that shed it," a passage in the Book of Numbers reads. In ancient Israel, murders and accidental killings of the innocent were avenged by the "redeemer of blood"—usually the victim's nearest male relative. Observing this retributive system saved the children of Israel endless blood feuds. Even domestic animals who caused a person to be killed were considered blood guilty and stoned.

And so the stalker in the shadows outside the abortion clinic might style himself a man of God.

There is an easy, baiting response to the question of whether state-sponsored vengeance is appropriate. One can simply cite the Pauline injunction: "Vengeance is mine, says the Lord, I will repay." But, to tell the truth, that would also be disingenuous. It evokes an image of a Rambo God, a gray grizzled hombre itching to get even. Keep your hands off him, boys, this one's mine. Can this tough-talking B-movie anti-hero, anxious to provide the director's money shot (head explodes in spray of blood), be reconciled with the God of Love?

Besides, Paul's letter to the Romans goes on to provide the following admonition:

> Every person must submit to the supreme authorities . . . For government, a terror to crime, has no terrors for good behavior. You wish to have no fear of the authorities? Then continue to do right and you will have their approval, for they are God's agents working for your good. But if you are doing wrong, then you will have cause to fear them; it is not for nothing that they hold the power of the sword, for they are God's agents of punishment, for retribution on the offender.

So to refer the asker back to his Bible would not be very helpful. Good Christians can support the death penalty. Executions are the law. Christians follow the law.

It is not so simple, is it? There is no surprise escape from this rhetorical trap, this devil's advocacy. It is absurd to expect an American politician to oppose capital punishment. That would require intemperate courage. Executions are barbarous and an inefficient use of the states' resources, and they are tremendously popular and indisputably legal. While it is possible to raise legalistic questions about whether this or that particular person deserves to be put to death, the advocates of killing criminals have tradition and law on their side. However impractical and inefficient this grim method of punishment may seem, it is an American custom. It is part of us, a clue to our national character. We are a people who have never been squeamish about spilling blood.

To resist capital punishment on moral grounds requires a certain arrogance. The best arguments against the death penalty—the most persuasive arguments—are practical arguments.

The death penalty consumes too much time and money, it is applied unfairly, it does not stop murder. It does not stop the nightmares of the victims' families. Mistakes are made, our judicial system is not perfect.

Executing a criminal might provide, for some, a moment of catharsis. A miserable death at the hands of the state punctuates what most certainly has been a miserable life. Perhaps these petty rituals satisfy the human yen for closure. Is that enough? We aren't required to kill.

Blood requites blood. Defiled land restored.

Camus thought that it must be easier for people of faith—people who believe in an afterlife—to rationalize capital punishment. For these people, execution is but a temporary sanction; only corporeity is burned away; indestructible soul rises or falls in accordance with the whims of God.

Yet Camus also recognized that all people—believers and atheists alike—have reached and maintained solidarity on one point; we stand together against human suffering and death. We are repulsed by the unnaturalness of murder. Whenever possible, we ought to be for less killing, less bloodletting. Every life has value, even that of the brute who would do us harm.

(1994)

World Gone Wrong

My Little Rock neighborhood resembles one of those London suburbs where private and council houses exist simultaneously, where stockbrokers live next-door to hairdressers and across the street from artists on the dole. I would reckon it is as diverse a neighborhood as can be found in Little Rock and perhaps in the entire state; our block accommodates a wide range of ages, income levels, and races. Our house is at the end of the street, with a stand of trees separating us from a railroad track. I look up from my desk and into a squirrel-riddled forest; I stand on my backyard deck and—because it is winter and the leaves are thin—I see the bathtub white dome of the state capitol. We have grown used to the wrack and whine of the trains; for us, it is quiet enough. And with our big dogs we feel safe enough.

But safety is an illusion in America, for every day there are moments when things go spectacularly wrong for someone somewhere. Newspapers catalog all the bizarre and sad things that can happen; our neighbors read the newspaper and don't feel as safe as we do. They worry that they will become victims, that rough men will come through their windows at night, take their things, and do them harm.

They are concerned because they believe there is a "gang house" in our neighborhood. At night, sometimes we see suspicious traffic, heavy old cars with gold chrome and blacked-out windows, sometimes with press-on luminescent letters spelling out odd words—"G-Thang," "Nomad"—along the top of the windshield or across the back glass. They cruise by the corner, gliding deeper into night, down the hill into the poorer reaches of our neighborhood, where we have little reason to go.

Sometimes at night, something cracks loud. The dogs bark. I get out of bed in the grainy dim and walk out into the back to quiet them. In the sky, I've seen a kind of cold glow, the moon behind a scrim of clouds, a reluctant witness to the evil that men do.

Guns and drugs. That is what it all comes down to—that and money, and alcohol, and meat.

Crimes occur mainly for economic reasons, and because the poor have so little to lose. It is easy to talk about the evaporation of moral certainties, of an eroding value system and the failure of ambitious social programs. It is easy to feel smug and superior when a Rush Limbaugh or an Ayn Rand gives you license to rage at lesser beings who cannot refrain from burning down their own neighborhoods or lighting up their crack pipes or pumping out their noxious music at antisocial levels.

No wonder so many people think the way to get at crime is to meet it in the streets, if not with your Curtis Sliwa-autographed baseball bat then with your draconian sentencing laws. Hardly a day goes by that someone does not call my office or send me a letter to promote the idea that if more people carried handguns and were prepared to kill this nation would be less violent.

Yes, there are reasons to be frustrated, for we live in what is by far the most violent country in the rich world. Most violent crime is caused by a small group of repeat offenders, many of whom serve only a fraction of their sentences before being released. No one in public life can afford to seem soft on crime, so it seems there will be no serious debate on proposed state and federal laws that would mandate lifetime terms for three-time felons.

Bill Clinton, seeing such laws proposed in thirty states— and already enacted in one—endorsed the idea during his first State of the Union address, delighting the Democrats and dunking right into the GOP's crime-fighting face. Never mind that incarceration has not proved an effective cure for crime, that housing prisoners in humane conditions is expensive, that prison overcrowding is already one of the prime reasons sentences are abridged, and that attached to each and every crime is a set of unique circumstances and individuals. Not all felonies are equal.

And the current American mania for mandate is in itself a troubling symptom of self-doubt. Why do we insist on term limits? Because we do not trust ourselves to turn the scoundrels out. On seat belts and motorcycle helmet laws? Because we do not trust our fellow citizens to look after their own self-interest.

On mandatory sentencing? Because we do not trust judges and juries to mete out appropriate punishments.

While we might grant that certain infringements on individual discretion are necessary, it is proper to instinctively resist such bloodless, mechanical formulas. Fear is what drives our capitulation to the machine; too many of us crave safety more than we love justice.

My neighbors do not worry for themselves as much as for their children. Bullets have no conscience, and every stray shot into the night comes crashing down somewhere.

It would be unfair to my neighbors to suggest that they cared less about this city's problems when crime was confined to certain other neighborhoods. It is one thing to read about bad things happening in the newspaper, quite another to realize that every other house on your block has been burglarized within the past year.

Of course you care more about proximate crimes; you grow sick of the precautions, of the screech of sirens in the night. There is a meanness in this world gone wrong; we worry that there are, among the shadows, a tribe of folks unmoored from the social contract, moving onto our streets.

I drove down the hill the other day, looking for the "gang house." I did not find it. I saw no outward signs of misbehavior. Perhaps the gangsters had been evicted—perhaps they were ghosts, projections of internal terror on the blankness of the ancient and oblivious night.

(1993)

Remembering Rebecca

She was a grayed-eyed girl with a short upper lip and dun hair she wore loose about her shoulders. Her usually fair skin had been rubbed the color of a bright penny by the Brazilian sun; her tiny teeth were colorless and straight, her features regular and fine. There was a bit of a child's skip to her gait, a kind of rocking shamble that bobbed her pretty head as she knocked along the sidewalks of Avenida Atlantica.

When she spoke her voice was money soft and husky, an alto touched lightly by a mid-Atlantic accent one might misidentify as British. It was a surprising voice for such a small girl; she was a true size two—delicate but not dainty. She lived with her parents in an apartment that required the entire fourteenth floor of a sleek glass building with a spectacular view of Ipanema beach. Like the other rich girls, she flew to Miami to buy her clothes and swore in French.

When I knew Rebecca in 1977, she was seventeen years old. She had just graduated from the American High School, and I was taking a break from college, recuperating in Rio de Janerio. She was a friend of my friend's sister, and I suppose that for a week or so we dated, though we didn't call it that. There was a group of about twenty of us—her friends, my friend's friends, mainly foreigners and graduates of the American school. We would have late suppers then collect in the designated bar or discotheque, pushing tables together and shouting over the music. We would drink *batidas*—made with sugar, fruit, and a cheap sugar-cane rum called *cachaca*—and Brahma Chopp, a sweet creamy beer, and dance until our clothes were soaked through. We would arrive in gangs and leave in pairs, and for a while, it seemed that Rebecca and I were always the only ones left at the table at the end of the night.

Rio was safe in those days, not as it is now. Drunken foreign kids could wander the streets without much fear, could climb aboard shuddering buses and pull at each other all the way home. This we did, night after night, infatuated with our lucky selves and our mutual adventure. We didn't talk much, for fear that talk would cripple the spell. What mattered most to us was barely expressible anyway.

• • •

I wish I could say I broke it off when I found out about Rebecca, but the truth is somewhat more awkward.

I knew she was an Afrikaner, a white South African of Dutch descent. I knew her family had an estate outside Johannesburg and that their stay in Brazil, while protracted, was merely a visit. I knew her family was rich and connected, that her father had held positions in the government.

Still, in Brazil, the tawny and the fair rode the same buses and ate in the same restaurants. Everywhere in the wicked and delighted city one could sniff the spiced scent of miscegenation. She never expressed any discomfort, she danced with men with faces black as Bibles. It was hard to imagine my friend a bigot, as ugly as any of the thoughtless hateful men I knew back home.

But she was. She told me so. It was a Saturday afternoon, and we were walking through the *Jardin Botanico*, near the Jockey Club, when I asked her about the peculiar institution of apartheid. I suppose I was needling her a bit; I know I expected her to be defensive. She wasn't. She told me flatly that she believed the black people of her country were "mere children," incapable of governing themselves. She told me how the Boers built South Africa; she pointed to the pitiful conditions in the rest of the continent to prove her point.

"The blacks are just intellectually incapable of running a country," she said. "Anyone who is honest recognizes as much. Look at your own country—what have the blacks ever done to build America? They are good musicians and athletes; they are jolly folk. But there are things that they cannot do; they are more spirit than mind. I have nothing against them, but they will never take our country from us."

It seems like we argued for hours. A part of me could never accept that she wasn't putting me on. At first I suspected she was parroting the shibboleths provided by her parents, that she was defending her country from what she felt was an uncalled-for, impolite attack. I told her what she was saying was nonsense and that I knew she knew it was nonsense.

She slapped my face and walked away.

And I'm still not sure whether I actually regret running after her, spinning her around, and apologizing—apologizing for being rude, not for being wrong.

I vowed not to talk politics with her, or anyone, ever again. I bought her flowers and a liquid silver chain from which dangled a carved jade fist—a Brazilian good-luck charm.

Yet something was extinguished that afternoon. She sensed it and would no longer slouch against me in the bars. I transferred my affections to someone else, a big-boned girl from Waco, Texas. Rebecca took up with a red-haired mountain climber, an older man who had his own apartment.

Rebecca and I were still friends, I suppose, but only in that odd way that people have when they have forgiven each other for something unspeakable. There was something ruined between us.

As it turned out, she left the country before I did, to go to school in Spain. When I got back to Louisiana, there was a letter waiting for me. She invited me to visit her in Barcelona. I wrote her back, enclosing a cassette recording of a song I told her I had written for her. She wrote me back, and I did not respond.

A couple of years later, a letter arrived for me at my mother's house. Rebecca was in Australia. I never wrote her back or even thought about her much—until last week, when her country was raked by bombings and by hope. I wish I'd kept up our correspondence. I wish I knew what Rebecca would say about the new country they are making in South Africa. We were friends so long ago, half her lifetime ago. We were children together. There was so much we didn't know.

(1993)

White-Haired Bum

December may be the grayest month, when the days contract from the cold like brittle steel, when shadows stretch and yaw. In the morning, you wake in darkness and crunch like Prufrock across dim grass, rubbing your hands together for heat. Breath comes in fine clouds, and you hunch over the steering wheel on the way to work and drive home with headlights groping through the early dark.

In December, you begin to feel the cold. It settles in your bones. Four weekends until Christmas, the candy lights come on and the malls become unpleasant. You want to sit at home, basking in the warm glow of ESPN, with your dogs and your *Beaujolais Nouveau*. Winter is not so bad, when you have a warm place to sleep and food to eat.

Of course, there are everywhere reminders that not everyone has a bed and a full belly. This is not the Reagan-Bush eighties, not Hard Times anymore. Now the economy is zipping along, we're into a recovery, but they still come at you in the street, asking for fifty-seven cents to fill out a bus ticket back home or a dollar and a quarter for a sandwich. The other day, in the lot where I park my car, across from the Deluxe Inn the prosecutors want to close because of the whores and the crack, there was a young woman, obviously worn-down but not badly dressed, who said she was a nurse on her way to take a job in Oklahoma, only her car had broken down and stranded her and her babies here in Little Rock.

Whatever you can spare, was all she asked. She said she was ashamed to beg, that even a few weeks before she could not have imagined herself asking strangers for money. But now it was what she had to do, so she trembled and stammered but she did it. You knew she was lying, that it was just one more artful scam, that there was no broken-down car full of babies. Or maybe you didn't know that. Maybe you thought she just might be telling the truth, that maybe she had exhausted all her resources.

Maybe you gave her something; maybe you just kept walking. When they come at you with their pleading eyes and extended hands, sometimes you look right through them. Maybe you hate the shell you've grown, the way you walk with purpose, your head up, your eyes bulletproof, the gruff way you shake your head and the soft, firm way you've learned to say "no."

There will be poor always, and you struggle to remind yourself there is no correlation between virtue and wealth. You know that the economy requires that there be people at the bottom, soft bodies to lubricate the gears. That's the way the world works; sometimes good people end up on the margins, beset by demons they cannot understand. A lot of people don't have much of a cushion—all that separates a lot of us from the streets is a paycheck or two.

But say you give them your change, or a dollar or five dollars? What does that do? At best it buys them a moment of comfort, a pint of cheap bourbon, a gas station hot dog. It doesn't help them, but maybe it makes you feel a little better about your enabling bourgeois self. You gave some bum a bit of change today; you are not all bad.

•   •   •

It was just a few days ago. He was half-feral, grinning dull, his head cotton-white, his mouth brimming gold. You could tell he was a little off, perhaps because his eyes were a little too kinetic for his head. He moved in stutters, shuffling and nodding, now bending his head to examine a shrink-wrapped cake in a shadowless convenience store.

I had seen him before, lurking beneath the viaduct where men sometimes camp. He was one of a group of men, squatting by the railroad track, where someone had thrown a rotten mattress. I felt like I knew him, in the vague way one knows a dog that roams the neighborhood. "White-haired bum" was how I thought of him, what I called him in my head.

As a shoplifter he was either very cunning or very stupid or just oblivious. He looked at me and opened the cold case, then lifted a package of luncheon meat and dropped it into the deep pockets of his long, tattered coat. He might have been using me as a screen, or he might have recognized me too and assumed that because our eyes had met that I would cover for him. He took another package, felt its heft, and performed the same operation. Then he smiled—sucking me into his toothy conspiracy—and turned his back and hunched to the rear of the cramped store.

I was startled, amazed, and more than a little jealous. I admit to an odd, grudging respect for people who do what they want to do, who shamelessly stuff things that don't belong to them in their pockets. It takes brass to steal—I found out early I had neither the hands nor the heart for it. If I were hungry and penniless, with no resources but my wit and wiles, I imagine I would starve.

So I envied this ragged man his capacity to steal—the coolness of spirit, the evenness of nerve—in the same perverse way one envies the brazen woman who huffs her way through the express lane with excess items, or the bow-tied bore who sends back the wine to impress some dull, unremarkable girl.

Some people can do what they want. The rest of us can only watch and seethe.

As it turned out I didn't have to decide whether or not to report my shadowy friend to the authorities. I would not have turned him in, but a man with a big flat voice and weary air of someone accustomed to dealing with petty thieves—the store manager, I guess—spoke from his perch at the counter. He never lowered his *National Examiner*.

"Put it back, chief. 'Else I'm going to have to call the police. Both pockets."

And the shoplifter put back the items, hanging them carefully on the very hooks they came from, with exactly the same shuffle and the same goofy, gold-flecked grin. No emotion, no charge of shame, nothing. Then he left.

There are, of course, reasons to steal. Some of us like to think we harbor a certain healthy impatience with convention, that we know society's rules are made to be broken and are broken everyday. Maybe aberrations are just boilerplate written into the genetic code. Too much conformity is stifling to the species—perhaps we need mavericks and wild-eyed southern boys more than we know. There might be honor among thieves after all; there might be a prick of jealousy in those of us too bloodless to take what we want and have it our own way.

When I was younger, I used to take ashtrays from hotels and restaurants. Because I wanted them to display as kitsch artifacts, because the places I took them from bothered to scratch their name deep in the pit. I saw maids scooting up the hallways, the ashtrays stacked on their carts, and I knew they were put out with the expectation they would be taken. I took them without shame, for their illicitness. It was nothing more than graceless pilferage, but I did it just the same. I don't think the places I stole from cared—I paid my bill, I felt entitled. They probably wanted me to take it.

That, I know, is not the point. The shoplifter's eyes were calmer when he lifted that junk meat than mine ever were when I palmed an ashtray. I did it strictly for the titillation, the same cheap excitement that makes some people drive too fast.

I paid for my gas and walked out to pump it. I watched the shoplifter scuff across the parking lot across the road and out of sight.

(1994)

The Suicide's Life

When he pulls you aside at a party you know it is something serious. He huddles with you and a couple of others to give you the news; someone you didn't know—someone that he knew—walked into the woods with a shotgun and did not come out.

Suicide is, among other things, an inconsiderate act. It engenders a certain social awkwardness. It causes good people to question their recent and remote interactions with the freshly dead. When someone you know kills himself, you recall every indifferent moment spent in his company, mining lost conversations for blunders and missed signals. Suicide is a blunt recrimination; every innocent heart indicts itself.

When someone you know knows someone who has killed himself, the best thing is to listen. Details don't matter, theories don't matter, and the dead one doesn't matter anymore. What matters is that your friend has been wounded, that a violent act has shaken him. However calm and Buddha-like your friend may appear, he has been roughed up.

"I'm at the point where I'm angry at him now," he says, and you can take this to be a good sign. Your friend knew the killer for more than twenty years, he worked with him, he knows his girlfriend, he never suspected, and yet it all makes sense.

"It's like he had written it down in his Daytimer—it's Friday, today I kill myself," he says, and something in the way he says it hints at resigned fatigue, the kind of letting go we settle for when the world goes wrong.

Let him talk. He describes a mild narcissist, a careful young man who watched his body and his money. He doesn't sound much different than a lot of us, and, of course, this act of self-annihilation seems preposterous—at least to a few folks sipping wine in a kitchen at a party.

"Some folks will not let themselves be held up to public ridicule," your friend says. "It's not that they can't, they just won't. They just say 'They will not do this to me.'"

That is what your friend thinks happened—that the prospect

of semi-public embarrassment drove his friend to suicide. He had messed up at work, and he might have lost his job. There might have been other consequences, maybe, probably not. It wasn't that bad.

Your friend thinks that's what happened, and that's good enough. He also thinks that's what happened with Vince Foster, that he simply decided he would not be an object of ridicule. It is an elegant answer, and maybe it is as good as any other. Maybe it is something we all would like to think—that not all suicides are capitulations, that some are acts of perverse courage and terrible will.

•   •   •

Is there a sane person who has not contemplated suicide? Probably not. We work ourselves into such twisted states; we all fumble and hurt. And it's not so far a step from imagining to doing as we like sometimes to believe. A twitch of the finger, a quick jerk of a steering wheel, and we'd be off, tumbling into the blistering light of the unknowable. What's extinction like, exactly, the state of nonbeing?

And any afterlife, could it be as blighted and difficult as this? Could it be as empty and pain-ridden? As delighting and limned with joy? As *real*?

All my trials, Lord, soon will be over. Crossing the bar. Zapping into some hyperspace special effects George Lucas Industrial Lights & Magic blur, a blizzard of pure energy, merged into that great collective consciousness, knowing all and why . . . .

Wandering cold, a pathetic lonely ghost. Disconnected, caught between worlds, the great unnoticed always looking in.

It's not for nothing these are great mysteries.

•   •   •

"Lucky" is the word for it.

He wasn't serious, though to be fair he probably didn't realize he wasn't serious. It was over some girl who had thrown him over for someone else, and after he took the sleeping pills and drank the cheap vodka he took a few minutes to call a few friends to say good-bye.

Of course, his friends got there in time, and the ambulance pulled up in front of the dorm to take him to the hospital where they pumped his stomach and the stern old priest came to visit him and told him he had narrowly averted spending eternity in the bad place.

A couple of days later, they sent the fighting-young-long-haired-priest-who-could-talk-to-the-young-people to visit him. Father Gary told him, in confidence, that the girl over whom he had almost done himself in was, truth be told, "kind of a slut" and certainly not worth the bother. And in a few days, he felt a little better and was properly embarrassed by the whole deal, the whole contrived, self-created, worthless, stupid thing.

His friends mercifully let him forget it after a few years, except for one of them who wrote about it in a newspaper column once.

He went on to be a healthy guy, a scientist and father, married to a wonderful red-haired woman whom he hadn't even known existed back in those angsty undergraduate days. He got to see Paris and to sit in a box seat at a World Series game.

Only a few friends and his mother remember him in that hospital bed, how pale and kitten-weak he was, and how the plastic identification band slid up and down on his wrist. Hospital light is never good light. That antiseptic scent stings your eyes and makes it look like you are crying.

•   •   •

There are lots of clichés about this business of living, a lot of stuff that people always say that are probably true. It is a hard thing to live in the world. There are all sorts of appliances that people use to try to stay in it. We need these things, these things like love and friends and wine. They are necessary. It is vain to pretend that we can know the mind of anyone else. We might know their hearts, but never their minds. When someone kills himself, perhaps the best thing to do is to mourn, and to understand that we are mourning for ourselves.

(1993)

The Cult of the
Good-Looking Corpse

At the end of 1980, I was freshly degreed and shopping for law schools. I was selling some free-lance album reviews, a few pieces here and there on pop musicians and their craft. I was playing rhythm guitar and writing songs for a self-conscious rock 'n' roll band, staying out late and drinking too much and generally doing my best to maintain an unregenerate pose.

When I think about those days, I invariably remember the amber, oily warmth of one particular club we used to play a lot and the way certain girls would toss their hair while they perched like exquisite, dumb, and fragile birds on high stools, pretending to play backgammon while actually—we were sure—scrutinizing us.

We were playing in this club on the cold December night John Lennon was murdered. We had just gone on break when we heard the news that he'd been shot, so we went right back on stage and announced it to our small crowd of friends. Then our keyboard player pecked out a tender version of "Imagine" on his Fender Rhodes and we packed up our gear.

My friend Pete and I went down to the Freeman Harris Soul Food Cafe, a joint that stayed open all night, and ordered a plate of fried chicken livers and a bottle of Jack Daniel's. We drank and we talked and I think we even may have laughed at the ridiculous grimness of that night. And in the only way available to shaken innocents trying to maintain tough-boy poses, I supposed we mourned.

We mourned a man we'd never met, whom we'd never hoped to meet. We mourned a man whose music, to be frank, meant less to us than we pretended.

We were, of course, caught up in the romance of death, in the bitter irretrievability of it all. A martyred Lennon served our purposes; we took to self-pity like the callow kids we were. His murder gave us a reason to drink whiskey and stare into that forsaken middle distance like Sammy Beckett's bestest boys. His murder seemed oddly beautiful in the same way that Kurt Cobain's suicide probably seemed beautiful to some of his fans.

• • •

Backstage, before a Christmas Eve concert in 1954, a Memphian named John Marshall Alexander Jr. placed a bullet in a chamber of his revolver, spun the cylinder, slapped it closed, put the barrel to his temple, pulled the trigger, and started it all.

Shuffle off the mortal coil, and another star is born. Ladies and gentlemen, please welcome the late, great Johnny Ace.

Death has historically been a great career move—ask Elvis next time you see him. Death can turn a sloppy mediocrity like Jim Morrison into a rascal god. Death can solve the world. It can validate your nihilism and soothe your teenage heartbreak and make the girl who never, in her self-absorbed petulance, gave you a soft thought, cry mascara-streaking tears at your funeral. Death can make you immortal, like what's-his-name from Joy Division.

Cobain apparently blew his own head apart with a shotgun. I can't begin to speculate on the reasons. Maybe he simply wanted, as his mother said, to "join that stupid club," the pantheon of rock casualties.

Suicide almost always seems stupid and selfish, but I don't know that any of us are immune to self-destruction. If a man like Primo Levi can hurl himself down the stairs after surviving Auschwitz, it's not surprising that punier hearts can succumb. It is sometimes a hard thing to live in the world.

I liked Cobain's music quite a lot. He expressed confusion and the impotent anger of disenfranchised youth as well as anybody has since the snotty Mick Jagger of the 1960s. His band Nirvana made a noise that was both stripped down and bombastic, a buzzy hell of big chords that married pop and punk tendencies. Cobain sang like a man trying to claw out of a grave.

It is no overstatement to say I love rock 'n' roll, that I find something thrilling in this simple music, inexpertly played. Rock has always been a game best played by amateurs. I adore its democratic heritage and its adolescent cheek.

But rock 'n' roll was a genre founded in blood and hype; there is something deeply disturbing in the cult of the good-looking corpse.

(1994)

McNamara

Silence. The red point of a cigarette glowing, then receding, then glowing again, a warning beacon in a darkened den. A father shuffling the smooth, worn deck of memory, smoking, sleepless, damaged.

It is late. Or early. It's morning, anyway, and even stumbling in after a ragged night in a rock 'n' roll bar, the kid knows enough to just walk on past this room, to let the old man alone with his old troubles and his can of beer.

He knows that this is no time to drop in and slouch down on the couch with his guitar case and long hair and try to affect a talking cure. He knows he hasn't got the words to calm these night sweats, that Dad will be all right in the morning, that the episode will pass.

So the kid walks on down the hall to his bedroom and flops on his bed in his jeans and running shoes. Because he's too wired to sleep he claps on a pair of headphones and notches up Bowie's *Diamond Dogs* until he feels like he can crawl into the shadowy reaches between the bass player and the drummer. Big notes pop in his head like antiaircraft fire.

Finally, he dreams of jungles and faceless mutants on Monster Island, his father running and falling through the bush, fires burning everywhere. When he wakes, he immediately loses the greater part of the dream—it's going even as he struggles to hang onto the final image. All the details, the vagaries of plot, evaporate like acetone, leaving behind only the scent and tang of the dream.

And the kid thinks that's what it must have been like.

The old man won't talk about it. About all he will say on the subject is that the ones who talk big, the ones who talk about killing and the fire fights and the report of the big guns, are either liars or fools. Real grunts never talk about it, not about the stuff they've seen. They just bear it.

There isn't anything to say about it anyway. Things happened, bad things, but there's no way to make sense of it. There was a whooshing sound and then the guy who was standing beside you just a second before was reduced to pink foam flecked on the tall grass.

What can one who was there say to one who wasn't? That they should be glad that they weren't there—that they shouldn't have been there?

That none of us should have been there.

• • •

Now that is the consensus. Vietnam was a mistake.

Robert McNamara has said so in a book. He says he wrote the book to explain to America why the dirty little war was prosecuted, why this nation's leaders acted as they did. He says he wants Americans to salvage the appropriate lessons.

"I want to look at Vietnam in hindsight, not in any way to obscure my own and others' errors of judgment and their egregious costs but to show the full range of pressures and the lack of knowledge that existed at the time," McNamara writes. "I want to put Vietnam in context."

As impossible as it seems to some of us, there are undoubtedly people out there who don't know McNamara was perhaps the key figure in the decision to escalate American involvement in Vietnam from 1961 to 1965. As secretary of defense, he was the primary war manager for both John F. Kennedy and Lyndon Johnson. There are people alive today who don't have a mental image of McNamara, who may not even recognize the name.

They don't have an image of him as some kind of banal accountant of death, a villainous technocrat crunching numbers and counting bodies as Westmoreland's war of attrition wore cruelly on. After LBJ, Robert McNamara was the one the protesters singled out, with his cool Ivy confidence and his map pointer: "The can-do man in the can-do society in the can-do era," David Halberstam wrote.

Now what are we to make of this *mea culpa*? That McNamara and his colleagues approached Vietnam with "sparse knowledge, scant experience and simplistic assumptions"? In their hubris, they viewed communism as monolithic and discounted the particulars of the historical relationship between China and Vietnam; they misjudged Ho Chi Minh's persistent nationalism and thought the South Vietnam government viable.

McNamara says he should have anticipated that bombing North Vietnam in 1965 would lead the South Vietnamese to request ground support. He says there should have been a public debate on the July 1965 decision for war, that government reports consistently misrepresented the situation to the public, that various peace initiatives foundered because "we failed to utilize all possible channels and to convey our position clearly."

We don't need McNamara to tell us a combination of wrongheaded confidence and bullheaded ignorance doomed the American misadventure in Southeast Asia. That much we could see. In retrospect, the very idea of "winning" in Vietnam seems fantastic, and the clique of suits who so long ago thought it possible seem as naive and faith filled as the apocalyptic sects that from time to time gather on mountaintops and in fields to await the imminent end of the world.

Vietnam might be viewed as one of the last imperial misadventures, a halfhearted attempt by the last superpower to prop up a corrupt client state.

It was a mistake. Three million Vietnamese and fifty-eight thousand Americans died, and soon there will be people out there to whom the whole bloody business in Southeast Asia will seem as remote as the signing of the Magna Carta, something historical and gray that happened before they were born. Yet even as we begin to forget it, it hurts.

Maybe the kid doesn't want to speculate on Robert McNamara's motives for writing this particular book at this particular time. Maybe he'll just forgive sad old McNamara, if that's what he wants. Forgiving him is not so hard to do. It was so long ago, and we were all crazy then. There is something decent and brave in an apology, no matter how late it comes.

The kid doesn't know how the old man might feel; he died young a dozen years ago, years after the fall of Saigon, after the last helicopter shuddered off the embassy roof. The kid still doesn't know what he did in the war, and he's not sure it's not better that way. The kid doesn't want to know.

Sometimes the only appropriate response is silence.

(1994)

Abraham Lincoln's
Cool Fire

In the 1950s, the composer Aaron Copland went to Caracas, Venezuela, to conduct a performance of his "Lincoln Portrait," an orchestral piece which features a narrator reading excerpts from some of the great man's most famous speeches and writings over a typically stirring Coplandic din.

"To everyone's surprise," Copland later told a newspaper reporter, "the reigning dictator, who had rarely dared to be seen in public, arrived at the last possible moment," and took a conspicuous seat among the six thousand spectators in an outdoor stadium. When the narrator—actress Juana Sojo—recited the final lines "government of the people, by the people—*por el pueblo y para el pueblo*—shall not perish from the earth," a minor riot erupted, with people jumping to their feet and cheering so loudly that Copland was unable to hear the final strains of music.

"It was not long after that the dictator was deposed and fled from the country," Copland said. "I was later told by an American foreign service officer that the 'Lincoln Portrait' was credited with having inspired the first public demonstration against him. That, in effect, it had started a revolution."

In this age of sound byte and gesture, it is difficult to imagine any American politician's words so thrilling a crowd. A hundred years from now will the ghost-written scripts of a Bill Clinton or a Richard Nixon or even a Jack Kennedy animate a fresh democracy in, say, Tripoli or Teheran? Of course not; words and ideals are secondary to the semiotic accouterments of the modern candidate; what affects our postliterate hearts is the way our president casts down his eyes and chews his lip, the way "Mister Newt" Gingrich brushes his hair back from his forehead. It is as if we live in a cave lit by lightning; we are dull beasts who apprehend the world in the flashes of electronic strobes.

Our world is different from Lincoln's; it's doubtful that a

man of his talents would today be drawn into the evermore technological arena of politics. The vulgar vocabulary of advertising has become our national literature. Glibness trumps reflection. There is no idea so clear and coherent that it can resist a hearty shouting-down.

That Lincoln was one of the five best writers this nation has produced is remarkable; that he could deliver long, complex, and compelling sentences was not. Nearly all politicians of Lincoln's day could write and speak well; the political culture of nineteenth-century America required its players to acquit themselves with pen and voice.

"Writing," Lincoln observed, ". . . is the great invention of the world . . . very great in enabling us to converse with the dead, the absent, and the unborn, at all distances of time and space."

Things have changed. Writing is a quaint and dying art. One imagines that homely Abraham—his face was, in Whitman's words, "so awfully ugly it becomes beautiful"—could probably resist the temptations of modern public life; he might well consider himself ill-equipped to compete with the ack-ack rhetoric of Bob Dornan and unprepared to suffer the ideological parameters installed by timid stage managers.

Not that politics has ever been the realm of secular saints. Things were rough in Lincoln's day as well, and Lincoln knew the limits of the possible as well as anyone. As polarized as we may seem now, our present arguments are trifles compared to the questions Lincoln tussled with—as George Will has pointed out, no wars will ever be fought over the appropriate level for the capital-gains tax. Lincoln was a politician—imbued with the requisite ruthlessness and ambition—but he was a transcendent politician and we occupy the country he saved for us.

Today there may be more enthusiasm for iconoclasm and debunking than hagiography; some of what Lincoln wrote can be turned against him by those unwilling to measure the dead by the standards that existed at their time. Some would deny Lincoln's greatness because he failed to anticipate the current vogue for "sensitivity" (which rushed in to fill the vacuum left by the evaporation of manners).

Others are simply lost in their own fractured times,

disconnected from history and tradition, cocooned in a solip-sistic web and fed by cables forcing light and sound. Lincoln is just the man on the penny, another obsolete artifact.

His cool fire is banked to embers, never dying, always avail-able to those seeking to spark a torch.

(1994)

He Never
Had It Made

Jackie Robinson and Brooklyn Dodger president Branch Rickey together ended baseball apartheid. In the process, they changed the character not only of the game but also of the nation. It is not so far-fetched to argue that Robinson's taking the field on April 15, 1947, inaugurated an era of civil rights progress for black Americans. Robinson's story is a most American story—and like most legends, it can be made to serve all kinds of different purposes. Most often it is reduced to a Horatio Alger homily: Robinson was given a break by Rickey and made the most of it, succeeding not only for himself but for the generations of black athletes who would eventually come to dominate America's playing fields.

But there are other ways to look at Robinson. He was a complex man—both a college graduate and a military veteran —when he first met Rickey. He was no mere jejune "boy" (a word he hated) to be formed and fired in the kiln of athletic competition.

Robinson was as prickly as he was courageous, and there was a bitterness to him that ought not to be ignored. He left baseball disappointed in 1957, and his "as told to" autobiography— finished as he lay dying in 1972—was fittingly titled *I Never Had It Made.*

In the book's foreword, Robinson wrote of his first World Series appearance, on September 30, 1947:

> There I was, the black grandson of a slave, the son of a black sharecropper, part of a historic occasion, a symbolic hero to my people. The air was sparkling. The sunlight was warm. The band struck up the national anthem. The flag billowed in the wind. It should have been a glorious moment for me as the stirring words of the national anthem poured from the stands. Perhaps it was, but then again . . . Today as I look back on that opening game of my first World Series, I must tell you that it was Mr.

Rickey's drama and that I was only a principal actor. As I write this 25 years later, I cannot stand and sing the anthem. I cannot salute the flag; I know that I am a black man in a white world. In 1972, in 1947, at my birth in 1919, I know that I never had it made.

Robinson's legend has obscured some baseball history. Most people probably believe that before Robinson stepped on the field with the Dodgers (after having integrated professional baseball a year earlier with Brooklyn's Montreal farm team) that blacks and whites had never played baseball together. This is not strictly true.

In the 1880s, a few black players were sprinkled throughout several professional leagues—including one who briefly played in a major league. Yet by the turn of the century, blacks were effectively banished from organized baseball. That happened largely because many white ballplayers, most notably Chicago's Cap Anson (now a Hall of Famer), refused to take the field with them.

And while racial hatred was certainly a motivating factor in banning blacks, purely economic factors should not be dismissed. Anson was talented enough to be assured a major-league contract no matter what the competition. But many less talented white ballplayers were more concerned that black players might take their jobs than with any indignity they might experience by playing side-by-side with them.

It is interesting that the banning of black players from organized baseball formally came up only once, in 1887 during a meeting of International League team owners. After a threatened strike by some white players, and a few ugly outbursts, the owners of the league's six all-white teams outvoted the owners of the league's four integrated teams and forbade black players.

But if the International League was the only professional league that put it in writing, soon all of organized baseball was lily white (the separate Negro Leagues wouldn't arise until after 1900) due to "gentleman's agreements."

Baseball's peculiar tradition was able to survive largely because of the way baseball leagues must necessarily conduct their business. For a league to survive economically, independent team owners must agree on how they will compete.

Teams act in concert to determine how players will be allocated, where games will be played, and a myriad of other details. In 1920, Congress affirmed baseball's special status by exempting the industry from the Sherman Antitrust Act.

Yet, as baseball history has shown again and again, the lines between cooperation and collusion are not always clear. It was especially easy for owners to close ranks on matters that could affect their bottom line. In theory, any owner who had wanted to put black players on the field could have done so.

But that owner would have risked not only turmoil in the clubhouse and possible fan boycotts, but also certain ostracism by his fellow owners. With Jim Crow then established in so many areas of American life, and not only in the South, it is hardly shocking that baseball owners were disinclined to disturb the status quo.

• • •

A convenient time to start the story of Robinson's breaking the color line is in 1942, when Branch Rickey moved from St. Louis to Brooklyn to become president and general manager of the Dodgers. The cigar-chomping Rickey was a man of ambition and real conscience—he broached the subject of baseball's color line early and often after taking the job.

At the time, Dodger policy was controlled by George C. McLaughlin, president of the Brooklyn Trust Company, which held 50 percent of the team stock. Rickey went to McLaughlin and told him he wanted to hold a meeting with the Dodgers' board of directors to discuss the mass scouting of players, including "a Negro player or two."

According to the legend, McLaughlin didn't flinch.

"I don't see why not," he supposedly told Rickey. "You might come up with something. If you find the man who is better than the others, you'll beat it. And, if you don't, you're sunk."

McLaughlin convinced the Dodger board to approve the scouting of black players. All the directors pledged themselves to secrecy about the "Negro Facet" of the Dodger plan, which Rickey suspected would not only lead to the breaking of the color barrier but also give the Dodgers a competitive edge in recruiting black players.

Rickey believed that once the first team signed a black

player, others were sure to follow almost immediately—and that the league's balance of power might be drastically affected by the influx of new talent.

Scouts were dispatched around the country to the diamonds of the Negro League. Dozens of prospects were considered, but in the end one name seemed to emerge from the pack. Jackie Robinson, a former UCLA football and basketball star, was playing for the Kansas City Monarchs. Robinson had some qualities that seemed ideal: he was a college graduate who had played on mixed-race teams in college; he had been an army officer; and he was still in his twenties (having been born in 1919).

On the other hand, the highly combative Robinson had barely escaped an army court-martial. While the popular version of the incident has Robinson being brought up on charges for refusing to move to the back of a civilian bus, he was actually accused of insubordination and "using vile and vulgar language" to a captain investigating that incident.

In his excellent 1995 book, *Great Time Coming*—a Robinson biography especially important for its portrayal of Robinson's life after baseball—David Falkner points out that Robinson sought the help of boxer Joe Louis and the National Association for the Advancement of Colored People in order to eventually win an acquittal. And though Robinson was found innocent, the incident did directly lead to his "honorable discharge" from the army "by reason of physical disqualification."

While it was apparent that Jackie Robinson was a fiery and intelligent man, not one to let a slight go unanswered, Rickey decided he was the best candidate. Scout Clyde Sukeforth was dispatched to Robinson.

"When Clyde Sukeforth said he represented the Brooklyn Dodgers and had come to the game specifically to see me play, I almost laughed in his face," Robinson later said. "I was sure that this fellow standing before me was just another crackpot."

On August 28, 1945, Jackie Robinson was standing in Branch Rickey's office.

The exchange has become part of American cultural lore, though there is at least a chance that Rickey and Robinson conspired to manufacture a myth. Still, while the truth is obscure, it does make for a very good story.

Robinson remembered that Rickey's first question to him was, "You got a girl?" He thought it impertinent, a "hell of a question." But he acknowledged that he did, and that he planned to be married shortly. Rickey approved, and told Robinson that he would likely need a good woman to rely on.

"Do you drink?" Rickey asked Robinson.

"No," Robinson replied.

"That's fine," Rickey said, leaning back in his chair. "Sit down. We have a lot to talk about."

Rickey told Robinson that he was primarily concerned with winning pennants in Brooklyn. World War II had depleted the Dodgers' playing talent, and for three years Rickey's team had been scouring the country looking for previously untapped sources of ballplayers, including the Negro Leagues.

Then Rickey came to the crux of the matter—was Robinson prepared to be a trail blazer? Rickey reached into his desk drawer and produced a book, Papini's *Life of Christ*, and began to read aloud the part where Jesus admonishes his followers to "turn the other cheek."

"Suppose you're playing shortstop," Rickey mused. "And I come down from first, stealing, flying in with my spikes high, and I cut you on the leg. As the blood runs down your shin, I grin at you and say 'How do you like that, nigger boy?'"

Rickey went on, imagining a World Series scenario:

"I'm coming into second with my spikes flying. But you don't give ground. You're tricky. You feint, and as I hurl myself, you ease out of the way and jam that ball hard in my ribs. As I lie there in the swirling dust, my rib aching, I hear the umpire crying, 'You're out,' and I jump up, and all I can see is that black face of yours shining in front of my eyes. . . . So I haul off and sock you right in the jaw."

At one point, Robinson is supposed to have asked, "Do you want someone who would not have the courage to fight back?"

"Robinson," Rickey is supposed to have said, "I'm looking for a player with the guts *not* to fight back."

And according to legend, Robinson signed a secret contract that day.

It makes for good folklore, and all three of the people present at the meeting—Sukeforth witnessed it—basically agreed on what had happened. But Robinson was too shrewd a man to have signed a contract minutes after it was presented.

Falkner believes that Robinson had met Rickey on at least two occasions before the August 28 meeting, and that Robinson was well aware of the situation when he showed up in Rickey's office that legendary day.

It is clear that, for the first three seasons he was under contract to the Dodgers (one with minor league Montreal and then two in Brooklyn), Robinson maintained an outward passivity unnatural to his character. He absorbed the taunts and even some physical punishment, retaliating only with his bat, glove, and spectacular base running.

In his fourth year, 1949, Rickey released him from his pledge.

"I could fight back when I wanted . . . ," Robinson wrote, "the principle had been established; the major victory won. There were enough blacks on other teams to ensure that American baseball could never again turn its back on minority competitors."

The Robinson experiment succeeded better than Rickey could have hoped. Not only did it force other teams to sign black players in order to remain competitive, but it also ushered in a Golden Age of Dodgerdom. In the forty-seven years before Robinson became a Dodger, the team had won five National League pennants. In the ten years he wore Dodger blue, they won six pennants (and finally their first World Series in 1955).

It is mildly surprising that Robinson turned out to be such a quality player, one who probably would have been elected to the Hall of Fame even if he hadn't been the pioneer who broke the color line. Robinson was a respected player, but hardly the best the Negro League had to offer. He had been playing professional baseball for only little more than a season when Sukeforth showed up.

"He wasn't the best player, but he was the best man," remembered Verdell Mathis, a former Negro League pitcher. "There was lots of men who could play like Jackie, some who could play better, but I don't know that there was another one who could have gone through what he went through."

•   •   •

Robinson and Rickey must share credit for breaking the color line. But Robinson's impact on the game was not merely sociological. From the beginning, he introduced a black aesthetic—the Negro League style of play—into baseball's major leagues. His syncopated dance off third base, his willingness to gamble when the stakes were right, upset baseball conventions and led to a rethinking of the game's conventional wisdom.

Robinson was an electric base runner who stole whenever he could—not just when circumstances dictated that he should. To those used to the stolid, home-run dominated baseball of the 1930s and '40s, his style could seem reckless and wild. The logic of Robinson's style was like the logic of jazz, not always discernible to those deaf to the nuances of the game.

Robinson used his athleticism to compensate for his relative lack of baseball experience. Although his swing was hitchy and unorthodox, hardly classic, he was more athlete than technician. He was an instinctive player, with an intelligence that challenged the pat assumptions baseball people reverently called "The Book"—decades before statisticians like Bill James were able to prove its fallacies.

Robinson's play was, in effect, a critique of and a challenge to the old brand of baseball, just as his blackness was a challenge to the old social order. Robinson was a harbinger of an important shift in American life. He was one of the first harbingers of a burgeoning black culture, held in check by legal and social stricture, that was about to burst forth and dominate the mainstream.

Robinson and Elvis Presley both *played black*. Both brought black style into the mainstream. And both were demonized as polluters before they were lionized as cultural heroes. Would Presley have been possible if not for Jackie Robinson? Perhaps, but it is probably more correct to see both Robinson and Presley as historical inevitabilities, as the first cracks in the cultural dam of the white massa's hegemony.

(1997)

• rants •

What We
Signed Up For

Since the earliest hours of our public presence, at the very dawning of our civic awareness, we have been alert to "our rights." From the first morning we appeared, scrubbed and buckled, in our elementary school classrooms, we have been assured of the specialness of our country, the United States of America.

Our first experiences with history were through the ritual-istic recitations of national myths and fables, stories distilled from actual events, but reworked and reordered so as to empha-size their moral lessons. We were taught to be little pilgrims and patriots, to prefer death to tyranny, to cherish a slippery ideal called "liberty," which might be best defined as the opportunity to enjoy those rights.

The America to which most of us pledged our allegiance was a simple, great-hearted land that could accommodate all colors, all creeds; a land that could, over a generation or so, smelt down the cultural differences between Gentile and Jew, between African and European, and deliver us all into a new land of equality of opportunity where we might be constrained only by the limits of our abilities.

We believed in a kind of American machine that was designed to manufacture a people of common values and uncommon tolerance. Its citizens were washed in the blood of various wars for independence and fortified by the divine covenant of the Constitution.

We grew older and maybe we learned about compromise and the imperfectibility of the human heart, and we learned to recognize the mythic symbolism for what it was. Yet we still felt confident that our America was the best country on earth in which to live.

We felt this, despite whatever specific disappointments we might have suffered at the hands of government, largely because we felt that "our rights" extended to us a protection that could not be abrogated by mere law. Rights have always been where Americans have joined the political discourse. They form the collateral of our social contract. While perhaps not an antidote to all manner of unfairness, at least these rights were rooted in something firmer than the statutory busy-ness of legislatures; our rights were handed down from a superior power.

While not a perfect document—it initially contained twelve amendments, two of which were never ratified—the Bill of Rights offers a splendid articulation of the expectations of the American citizenry. It affords us innocents with a firewall against the excesses of government. Its elegant Ninth Amendment—the enumerated powers clause—allows the judiciary to accommodate societal evolution. It allows for the imagining of rights not specifically listed in the Constitution—a right to privacy, perhaps—and implies that while individual rights may be expanded, they can never contract.

The Ninth Amendment anticipated that the America of 1996 would not be the same as the America of 1791; indeed, America is not the same today as it was when we first cupped our hands over our hearts and faced the blackboards.

●　　●　　●

In many ways, America is better.

On the radio the other day Rush Limbaugh was heard lamenting that newspaper headlines no longer refer to America's "enemies" in blunt words; we no longer refer to the Japanese as "Japs" and—thanks to the implosion of Soviet communism—the term "Reds" has been reclaimed by the Cincinnati baseball club. While Limbaugh and his ditto-mongers might think this is bad news, it is a change with which most of us can probably live.

The inevitable advances in technology have proved more liberating than enslaving. Orwell's Big Brother has not materialized; instead, personal video cameras catch the authorities at their abuse and the Internet allows every voice to publish. Education has eroded much of the innate prejudice we all hold toward Otherness. Our lives are generally more comfortable, if not of higher quality.

We have the luxury of arguing about silly things; of spending millions of dollars to investigate this politician and that one. We have developed the capacity to make an entertainment out of anything, to hoot and cheer along the internecine battles of congenital politicians and pompous old liars.

And yet the prevailing note in the national chord is fear. Where de Tocqueville found us hardy and ingenuous, a modern visitor could not help but notice the fear-stink on our clothes. Freed—at least momentarily—from the threat of nuclear annihilation, we have turned the loathing inward. Lenny Bruce warned us of as much; when the Commies went away we began hating each other.

It seems we cannot help but be afraid of AIDS, of crack gangstas, of environmental catastrophe, of dirty pictures masquerading as art and of art disguised as smut. We must keep our office doors open whenever a person of the opposite sex visits; we must watch our mouths and not allow those lascivious thoughts to find purchase in our fallow brains.

We are afraid of teenagers and the boomy music they carry on their shoulders, of murderous mundanity in the street and unorthodox loving in the bedroom. We are afraid of the people who turned loose O. J. Simpson, of the jack-booted thugs who might at any moment bash down our doors and pry away our cold dead fingers in order to confiscate our guns.

We are afraid of Hillary Clinton and her big high hairdo, of the tin-pot Torquemada Alfonse D'Amato, of Oliver Stone and his loopy obsessions, and God knows we are afraid of the Truth.

We have bartered off our rights in exchange for an illusion of security that doesn't make us feel any safer; we've allowed damage to the infamous Fifth Amendment, and we've totally cashed in the Fourth in order that Drug Task Force Agencies might ride around in shiny black four-wheel-drive sport utility vehicles and arrest great wads of cash.

We live in a country where buying an airline ticket with cash makes you a suspected drug dealer, where if your cheating no-account husband picks up a prostitute in the family station wagon that you yourself bought and paid for, and gets caught by the cops in some tawdry Hugh Grant deal, the cops can take the car.

We fear the government, and so we allow it to incarcerate more and more of our fellow citizens. In the current climate, police can do whatever they want to almost anyone they want so long as they can imagine some legitimate reason why they might want to do it; doctors are forbidden from discussing all possible options with their patients; legitimate businesses are unable to advertise their products; courts have begun to issue orders restraining the publication of books and the broadcast of news—and the list of restrictions placed on individual behavior has grown depressingly long.

This isn't what we signed up for, folks.

(1995)

The Guerrillas
in Our Midst

The day after the Oklahoma City bombing, Rush Limbaugh went on the air and railed at the people he and other Americans assumed were responsible for the murders.

"You dogs, you cannot hide! And when you are found, it will be the worst day you can possibly imagine!" Limbaugh said. Then, he turned almost wistful as he addressed his listeners.

". . . And if we trace it to a particular nation, what about hitting the nation anyway, even if we don't know who exactly did it?"

Perhaps we shouldn't blame Limbaugh for engaging in what, in retrospect, may seem irresponsible rhetoric. A lot of us thought the same things; the airwaves were thick with rumor and innuendo and bits of information that seemed to point toward foreign involvement in the bombing.

My own initial gut guess that the perpetrators were probably homegrown white supremacists striking a blow against what they habitually refer to as the Z.O.G.—the Zionist Occupation Government—was quickly amended when I realized how effective and competent the bombers had been. Frankly, I didn't think the local boys had it in them to pull off something so big. They could handle a smaller bomb, one that might take out a dozen or so people, but something like what happened in Oklahoma seemed to me beyond their ken.

I thought it was "Middle Eastern terrorists," too.

And when it turned out that it looked like kooky "patriots," buried in the shock and horror was a slim beam of relief. As bad as it is, it would be worse to think that the Islamic jihad or Hamas had penetrated so deep into this nation's guts that we might indeed be forced to scramble planes and to drop bombs and cause collateral damage of our own. We are xenophobic enough; had the bombing been blamed on "Middle Eastern terrorists" thousands of innocent Americans, as well as foreign students and other resident aliens, would have suffered. When it became clear that the investigation was being focused on domestic terrorists, an editor at this newspaper, in typically dry newsroom style, allowed that "if you've got any Arabs tied up in your basement, you'd better let them go."

Better also let go of the notion that only those of another culture and national temper could have done this terrible thing; better let go of the hubris that keeps us from seeing that evil has its purchase in the heartland. Better let go of the idea that these guys who paint their faces black and dress in camo to crawl around in the woods or the desert playing soldier are just irrelevant wackos.

In recent days, a lot of people—including the president—have suggested we examine our escalating anger, the swaggering rhetoric that permeates some radio talk programs, the Internet, and sometimes Congress. Some people worry that hosts like Chuck Baker in Colorado incite marginal people to violence. "You never know whether there's some fragile person who's out there about to tip over the edge thinking they can make some statement against the system—and all of a sudden there's a bunch of innocent babies in a day-care center dead," Clinton said.

Francisco Duran, the Colorado Springs militia man accused of pumping more than thirty shots at the White House, is a self-professed fan of both Baker—who has advocated "cleansing" the government of "slime balls" in Congress and bureaucrats "who are too stupid to get a job"—and Limbaugh. I remember how queasy I used to get when I'd hear Bob Mohan in Phoenix talk about "putting down" handgun-control advocate Sarah Brady.

Limbaugh is a Republican partisan, not an extremist. But there's a fine line between rhetoric and incitement, and even some congressional voices have lately pushed the boundaries of civil discourse. If you genuinely believe the federal government has lost its moral legitimacy, then aren't you compelled to resist its encroachments on personal freedoms?

Actually, we ought to proceed very cautiously before we clamp down on speech of any sort. Scurrilous talk radio programs and magazines such as *Soldier of Fortune* serve a legitmate function in our society—like pornography they harmlessly gratify certain unseemly appetites that might otherwise be manifested in dangerous ways.

• • •

A friend sent an e-mail message a couple of days after the bombing. He was stunned and weary. He said it hurt to realize that the bombers were likely American kids, rural folks who'd just heard that familiar tattoo of "less government, less government."

"It could have been me," he wrote.

No, it couldn't have, hoss. Not in a million years. These are cracked creatures. We've known about them for years; occasionally we hear them leaking into the AM airwaves with their paranoid whining about black helicopters and the "New World Order" that they see as an attempt to impose a one-world government. I've been in their silly bookstores and looked at their scary boom-boom magazines. Addled boys, most of them, guys who love too well the satisfying click of a precision mechanism and the charmed heft of a handgun. You ain't like them.

Cowardly little stunted souls who wait in their cellars surrounded by cases of powdered milk and boxes of bullets, for the day when they—thank God Hallelujah—will actually have cause to defend themselves and their families just like Saint Bernie Goetz. Guys who figured they'd had a chance to be somebody if it wasn't their dumb luck to be born white and male and American near the end of the twentieth century, guys who really could have cut it in the days before cable television turned everybody's mind to mush and before rap music and crack cocaine turned the negro into an urban predator.

Edwin Arlington Robinson, one of the better bad poets to stumble out of New England, had their number: *Miniver Cheevy, child of scorn, cursed the day that he was born . . . .*

Most of these bitter guys are just in it for the beer and the comradeship. As a friend of mine said, most of them hooked up with these groups because they couldn't afford the dues down at the VFW. If it ever came down to actually putting themselves at risk, if the Russian troops that some of them believe are already on U.S. soil ever kicked in their door, most of them would make terribly ineffective guerrillas—because they are terribly ineffective people.

But there are apparently a few who are capable of murdering defenseless office workers and children.

(1994)

A Pornography
of Guns

On the morning President Clinton signed the Brady Bill into law, I went to a gun store, just to look at the handguns.

They were still there, of course, in sooty gray-black or blued or nickeled or in stainless steel, each a variation on the Ideal Pistol, the mythic American equalizer. Under the rapid flutter of fluorescent light, they glint like so much cold and precious jewelry, latent and safe as snakes behind museum glass.

I am drawn to this display, to these Brownings and these Colts and Sigs and Pietro Berettas, to their tight tolerances and military nomenclature, their offhand precision. It would be a lie to deny that they are beautiful.

I watch with something like envy as a salesman explains something esoteric to a customer who has brought his pistol in for repair. The salesman takes the gun and works the action, then hands it back over the counter to the customer. Not quite by chance, I overhear the customer's remark: "Oh, so it's a gravity thing."

So it is. Whenever you pick up a pistol for the first time, or after not having handled one for a long time, invariably you will be surprised at how much it weighs. There is something good about a handgun's peculiar heft, something at once attractive and scary and fine. It is a solemn weight, for a gun is an instrument designed to kill. And there is something about men and guns; there is something frail in us that makes us want them.

I have been thinking a lot about guns these past few months. Leaving aside the deeper psychological questions—I suspect the Freudian metaphor is in many cases appropriate—it is hard to imagine the South without pickups fitted with racks and dens with glassy, locked-down cabinets. Our guns are a part of our way of life; a father's Christmas gift of a rifle to his son is freighted with expectation and initiation. There is a part of me that loves guns, a part of me that believes that part of being a man is knowing and caring about guns.

But I also know that this is a bloody country, perhaps the bloodiest in the world. I've heard the surprisingly tiny, percussive snap of small arms fire at night, and I have seen the bodies of children murdered by children. Violence is an intransigent part of our national character. And maybe, as the mantra goes, guns don't kill people. But people die because other people shoot them with guns. Or because they shoot themselves with guns. Whatever else, handguns make it easier to kill.

• • •

A dozen years ago, I went shooting fairly often with my friends from the Jefferson Davis Parish Sheriff's Department. We would drive into the south Louisiana forest, to deep clearings where we'd set up paint cans and pop bottles. Then they would break out the weapons, the *Dirty Harry* pistols and the riot shotguns, and we would roar away. I remember the thrilling shock and fulmination of a fully automatic weapon in my arms. I remember what it was like to think a beer can in half, to have it done almost as quickly as I thought it. An Uzi burst was reflexive, mild as a warm shudder in the bicep, and powerful enough to bust apart a log.

It was fun to stand there in the woods with my friends and run through boxes of ammo, with the sweet stench of powder mingling with our sweat. I am tempted to say that in those moments we never thought about killing, about the things our toys were made for, but my friends were lawmen and I am sure their private thoughts must have been different, more serious, than mine. I took a simple delight in the tinkery, in the just-so adjustment of the sights and the solid, oily thunk of metal upon metal.

It was only later that I wondered at myself. Could I level a gun at something animate? Could I squeeze the trigger? If I were angry or threatened or afraid enough? I don't know, but I fear that I could. Sometimes, when my temper shows, I think it is a good thing that I don't own a handgun, that I might flash it at the inconsiderate and stupid. Just to let them know the world is not always a tolerant place.

Passing fantasies, but some people act on them. A friend and I were walking into a nightclub in Phoenix one night when we passed a man who had just pulled his BMW up to the curb at an odd angle, so that it took up more than one parking space. "Nice job of parking," my impolitic friend offered. The man said nothing, but stared at us and with his left hand opened his jacket, revealing a big silver gat. We kept walking.

That was in the big city. But I've seen guns flashed in Little Rock as well as in smaller towns. A few years ago I was in a small town in south Arkansas, in a part of town notorious for its crack trade, and I apparently drove too slowly past or looked too hard at a pair of young men in the street. One of them lifted his untucked shirt to show me he was packing.

Chairman Mao got it wrong. It is not political power that blooms in the barrel of a gun, but individual power. A man with the gun is entitled to, if not respect, at least deference, whether he's dressed in ragged sweats or evening clothes. A gun is most powerful as a tool of negotiation—people with guns can choose their own way until their guns are met by other guns.

I am resistant to the idea that there is more and more badness in the world. I try to maintain a Roussean faith in the inherent morality of human beings. People are not any more monstrous than they have ever been, but the technology has improved.

In "Defining Deviancy Down," a recent essay in the *American Scholar*, Sen. Daniel Patrick Moynihan argues that we have become inured to what, thirty years ago, would have been considered an intolerable level of crime. Moynihan's prime example is the St. Valentine's Day Massacre, in which seven gangsters were murdered by other gangsters. That event was considered so horrific that it merited two entries in the *World Book Encyclopedia*.

It is easier to kill than it has ever been before. While fourteen-year-olds used to duke it out with their fists, now school kids blaze away at each other. If MTV can be believed, in some places even good kids are now carrying handguns to school. One fell out of the knapsack of a quiet, studious type, and rattled down the stairwell of a New Orleans' high school. Over Thanksgiving, a bright thirteen-year-old told me that while he was enrolled in a local junior high school, the authorities occasionally found firearms in lockers and book bags.

And, this is the most important thing, there is something impersonal about shooting a handgun. Physically, it is difficult to fight another person, to draw them close enough to smell their breath, their sweat, their fury. Most people draw back from such close confrontations; the fear of being hit back is a strong deterrent—and even when one is "fighting for one's life" there is a tendency to pull one's punches, to mitigate the damages to that other, struggling person.

Twice as an adult I have fought hard. Once, in Chicago, a boy tried to mug me. I was bigger and quicker than he, and when he confronted me in the foyer of the apartment building, I was able to kick the door so that it trapped him against the jamb. For a moment, long enough for me to throw a couple of wild, teary-eyed punches, he was helpless. I suppose that if I had been more ruthless, and less terrified, I could have done him some serious injury. But I backed off and let him run back into the night.

Then, a couple of months ago, while my wife and I were walking our dogs, they were attacked by a pair of boxers. I peeled them off my dogs and wrestled with them—I finally even kicked one of them—but again my internal governor only allowed me to go so far. I didn't hurt the boxers, though I was scared and as angry as I can ever remember being. I think if I had had a gun with me I would have shot that would-be mugger. I know I would have shot those dogs.

Macho poses aside, to knife or strangle someone requires a brutal intimacy. Certainly we are capable of killing each other this way—Cain slew Abel—but it is psychologically and practically more difficult. A handgun can kill from across the room or across the street; a bullet never has to overcome its victim's cries. The whole purpose of a firearm is to make killing easier and safer.

So ask the people who own handguns why they keep them. Invariably, they answer "for protection." That's why my father kept a loaded .38 in his nightstand, why burly pro football players carry them, and why skinny high school kids who wear their baseball caps backward pack.

I don't know how things escalated, but I know that a few years ago I was sure that having a handgun in one's house was a reckless thing. I still think that statistics show that guns are more dangerous to gun owners than to anybody else, that they are more likely to be stolen by criminals than to thwart them, and that a great many people who own guns are not emotionally or morally prepared to own them. But it is a scarier world than it was a few years ago, and there are honest people who disagree with me. They have their own statistics, their own pet theories about the trajectory of crime and the efficacy of gun-wielding citizens in combating it.

They may be wrong, but I wouldn't take away their guns.

•   •   •

One of the more distressing characteristics of our age is the polarization of discourse, our inability to hear each other. Americans have been balkanized into interest groups, each with its own catechism. This leads to many strange inversions of decorum, as when self-proclaimed "pro-lifers" celebrate the murder of an abortion doctor or when "liberals" attempt to force college students into the mental straitjacket of political correctness. There are moral absolutes, but there are gray areas also, and the question of whether a law-abiding person ought to go down and purchase a handgun without any restrictions is one of these gray areas.

Guns are dangerous, as dangerous as automobiles. It seems reasonable that their use be subject to at least some regulation, that the state has a legitimate interest in ensuring that those who own them are mentally sound, that they have not exhibited any propensity for serious misbehavior, and perhaps even that they know something about how guns operate and how they may be operated safely.

But many gun owners disagree; they see gun ownership as a natural right, conferred not by the state but by God. It is, after all, right there in the Constitution, albeit fettered by that archaic bit about the militia. True Jeffersonians worry that if guns are outlawed, only the government will have guns. I think these worries are legitimate.

I also think that gun-control battles will not be won by statistics, though both sides have their champions. On a couple of occasions in recent years, I have spoken with Gary Kleck, a Florida State University criminologist whose statistics show that privately owned handguns *are* effective in fighting crime. Kleck's statistics fly in the face of the accepted wisdom—and just about everyone else's statistics—but I believe he is sincere, and that he did not set out to become the National Rifle Association's pet academician.

Kleck's studies show that everything I used to believe about gun ownership is wrong. He found that the class of people who owned the most guns, the old and the wealthy, were decidedly less violent than the class of people least likely to own guns, the young and the poor. Kleck claims that over 4 percent of households in the United States have used a gun defensively—to scare or fight off a criminal—in the past five years. He claims that in any given year, more than a million Americans will use a gun to successfully defend themselves against criminals. According to Kleck, handguns are twice as likely to be used to defend against criminals than to be used in the commission of a crime.

Yet while Kleck seems sincere—he says he is no fan of the NRA and is a member of the American Civil Liberties Union and that he was surprised by his findings—I don't believe his statistics. But neither do I accept those of such groups as Sarah Brady's Handgun Control, or the Violence Policy Center, however well-meaning these groups may be. When Marjolijn Bijlefeld, the associate director of the National Coalition to Ban Handguns, argues that "people are better off having a telephone or a German shepherd than owning a handgun; they're just as effective and much safer," she is probably telling the truth. But people are better off not smoking and not eating red meat. Guns may not be the best way to provide home protection, but they are an option.

Though everybody has a study to buttress their position, the numbers are finally as irrelevant as they are elusive. No one will be convinced by spreadsheets, but everyone has their favorite. Take, for example, a 1981 Justice Department report called "Weapons, Crime and Violence in America," conducted by James Wright and Peter Rossi, two sociologists at the University of Massachusetts.

Both their report and subsequent book, *Under the Gun*, state that they found "no compelling evidence that private weaponry is either an important cause of or deterrent to violent criminality." That may be closer to the truth than the shrill voices on either side of the debate. Increased firepower is more responsible for the increase in casualties than the existence or prevalence of guns. That Uzi I cradled a dozen years ago was an expensive and relatively exotic weapon—these days you can pick them up in pawn shops. A Tech Nine—a 9 mm gun with a big clip preferred by many "gangsters"—retails for just a little over two hundred dollars and can be had for less than half that on the streets. One of the most attractive features—the big selling point—of the Tech Nine is that it resembles a machine gun.

•   •   •

Bill McIntyre, the director of communications for the NRA, says the ranks of his organization have been swelling since the Los Angeles riots in the wake of the Rodney King beating. He claims the NRA is gaining members at the rate of fifteen hundred to two thousand members a day. "In general, they're coming to us out of fear," McIntyre said. "Fear for their own safety—and there's the realization that the NRA is the only game in town—fear of the potential loss of rights. Now we have an administration that's obviously hostile to the idea of private gun ownership."

For their part, the NRA protests that gun control doesn't keep criminals from obtaining guns and—considering the number of weapons already floating around the country—they may have a point. Handgun Control claims there are already more than one hundred thousand rapid-fire machine guns in private hands in this country. Stopping the sale and importation of such weapons wouldn't cause those guns to disappear.

Still, the relatively small number of people killed by handguns in countries with strong gun-control laws is something to consider. In 1990, when handguns claimed the lives of 10,567 Americans, only 22 people were killed by handguns in Great Britain; 13 in Sweden; 91 in Switzerland; 87 in Japan; 10 in Australia; and 68 in Canada.

What strict gun control may do is deter many law-abiding people from buying guns. That, in itself, is not a bad thing—for the "law abiding" kill themselves and their family members, leave their weapons out where kids can get them, and have them stolen. Gun control may be inevitable, but not because the NRA is losing its battle of angry words with other special interests. Gun control is inevitable because the people caught in the middle, the people who subscribe to no pro- or anti-gun orthodoxy, will become weary with crime and impatient with their government. They will demand strict controls on the sale of handguns.

That is not necessarily what should happen, but what will happen. People invariably trade freedom for safety; that is why we have no smoking zones, motorcycle helmet laws, and seat belts. Someday, handguns will be contraband, but there will still be bad people in the world. And maybe a new machine for killing.

●   ●   ●

Guns are beautiful, but they are also ugly, and a pornography has grown up around them. There are certain gun shops that cultivate an air of fetid illicitness. Some trade in cheap, mean-looking guns that pander to the immature appetites of insecure people. Some also sell beepers or brutal knives. There is a frightening subculture of would-be mercenaries, snipers, bounty hunters, and professional murderers.

Ultimate Sniper, a videotape sold by Paladin Press (they also publish books that provide detailed instructions for stealing cable television, perpetuating check and credit fraud schemes, and, perhaps most intriguingly, *How to Disappear Completely and Never Be Found*), features a conversation with former marine sniper Carlos Hathcock, who at one point talks about "dumping" his human prey:

> You know where you have to shoot the bad guy to do him in right quick. That's in the head. But I ain't going to do that at 700 yards. No way in a cat hair. . . . You got nineteen inches from your waist to your chin to shoot in and twelve inches across. You got a big space there, a big space. To get everything correct you should shoot him right in the middle. Your heart's not on the left like everybody says it is. It's in the middle.

There's no obvious way to gauge how pervasive the market is for this sort of stuff, but most grocery store magazine racks— which do not have space for such general interest, mainstream publications as *Harper's* and *Atlantic Monthly*—do carry journals dedicated to handguns. Some of these are apparently serious and relatively sober, but there are others—such as Larry Flynt's *S.W.A.T.*—that are thoroughly creepy.

Apparently targeted at professional gunmen, a typical one-hundred-page issue of *S.W.A.T.* includes dozens of pages of firearm-related advertising—some of a highly dubious nature. In its pages one can find advertisements for books and videotapes which purport to offer training in "action careers" as bouncers, stuntmen, and private investigators, as well as instruction in "street fighting" and "expert combat," as well as an ad for a device called the "Hydra Ram," the "first and only one-piece integrated forcible entry tool." Or you can send away for your own photo identification kit, which will allow you to make your own "special weapons permit," "mercenary credential," or "international driver's license." And of course there are lots of photos of vicious-looking weapons, laser sights, and plastic knives.

On the editorial side, the magazine offers the standard "advertorial" pieces on weapons manufacturers (usually some specialty factory in Finland), legal advice columns ("Can Cops Carry Switchblades?"), and "practical" instruction ("The Brain Stem Shot: Are We Being Needlessly Precise?"). Who reads this stuff? Probably the same kind of frustrated young men who peruse Flynt's other publications, looking for images with which to furnish their fantasies. No policeman I've ever known would read such trash, though plenty of policemen take a professional interest in weapons. I'm sure some genuine gun enthusiasts flip through *S.W.A.T.*'s pages—either for amusement or to look at the ads. And there are probably a few truly dangerous nuts on its subscription lists.

●　　●　　●

It is important to remember that most people who are deeply interested in handguns are not interested in gun smut. People like Max Cloninger, who owns the Heights Gun Shop in Little Rock, are as disgusted by that kind of thing as any slouching, sensitive reader of the *New Yorker*. Cloninger employs off-duty policemen in his shop, sells only high-quality weapons, and keeps meticulous records. His advertising is cast toward hunters. Still, he sells more handguns than anything else—he estimates that 70 percent of his business comes from people who are buying handguns for self-defense. These people are interested in guns not because they are caught up in the romance of ordnance, but because they are worried about their families. These are practical and substantial people who worry about safety and hope they never have to fire their guns anywhere other than the pistol range. Many of them would consider themselves social liberals, but they still want to be ready when Scary Bob climbs through the window. You can tell them their idea of security is wrongheaded, but you will not convince them—they've thought about the problem and come to their own conclusion.

●   ●   ●

I know a young man named Jeff Blaine who works at a very trendy downtown pizza restaurant. Jeff is bright, with regular features framed by shoulder-length hair. He is pleasant to talk to. He is the kind of cheerful young person one often sees selling jeans or soft drinks on television, fashionable and unthreatening. He is also a member of the NRA.

He wants, someday soon, to move to the West, to the mountains, and work as a gunsmith. He has a school in Colorado picked out. All he needs to do is save up the money to go. There is nothing nutty about him. He argues against gun-control measures at least as surely as anyone could suggest arguments for the measures. He has learned his catechism; he can cite his stats. There are other stats that he ignores, but that's the way these things are argued.

But even as we talk, we both know there is something more to guns than what we're talking about. They may be tools, but they aren't just tools; they are horrible and they are glorious. Guns gave us America to live in, and guns pose the biggest threat to the American way of life. They are serious things. Jeff likes to make the point that a citizenry acquainted with the care and feeding of firearms is better equipped to resist tyranny than a meeker people. Who could disagree?

I guess that I don't mind anyone keeping guns, not even handguns. I just want them to be sober about the business. And from the number of shot-pitted signs I see on rural roads, the number of bad things that I see written about in the newspapers,

I know that this is too much to expect. I cannot speak for everyone, but I know that the part of me that wants to own a gun is a weak and irresponsible instinct, like the part of me that craves a motorcycle. And while it has become a trite truism to say that a gun is not a toy, for most of us that is exactly what it is.

There is nothing intrinsically noble about handguns; though one can admire the precision and the sweet workings of the things, the ultimate purpose of them is to extinguish the inexplicable intelligence of life. That is what they are made for, and there is lethality in their odd weight. Maybe that is why a gun feels heavier than it looks; the taking of life, even the life of a rattlesnake or a fiend, ought to be a weighty thing.

(1993)

Limbaugh Nation

In America, we are all addicts in various stages of degradation. Some go for crack, some for C-SPAN, some for the adrenal juicing they say parachuting supplies. Among my several weaknesses—by no means my chief one—is a fondness for listening to talk radio.

I must watch my diet, for too much talk radio can make you crazy, even when that talk radio is filtered and scrutinized, ginned of obvious cranks and hate freaks. Even on a professional show, the level of discourse is often distressing. When guests are rare and callers are not vetted—and that is the practice of at least one Little Rock radio station to which I regularly listen, a station which takes a perverse pride in not screening callers—listeners are often presented with a grim biopsy of yahoo culture. And while I know—or, to say it more accurately, *hope*—that callers to talk radio programs are not representative of talk radio listeners, much less the nation at large, it's dispiriting to hear the moral confusion and inappropriate rage of this vocal minority.

I shouldn't listen, but I do: There is something raw and scared in the voices of these Americans who so desperately hate Bill and Hillary Rodham Clinton, who believe this country would be a better place if, like Singapore, we occasionally caned malefactors, and who think that more guns in the hands of more people is the key to controlling crime. I marvel at their meanness, their unskeptical acceptance of arcane conspiracy theories, and their willingness to automatically attribute the worst motives to those they consider their enemies.

I admit my thrills are voyeuristic and shameful, and I even wonder if there's not an element of misuse in my listening. I strive to remain ironically detached from the proceedings; I do not expect to hear anything I can put to later use or that will make me a better person. I listen less for entertainment than out of a kind of jaded, anthropological fascination.

I'm sure the callers—and the hosts—wouldn't appreciate my attitude of bemused condescension. But I also assume it's exactly what they expect from the likes of me.

•　　•　　•

One tries hard to understand the anger. The First Amendment is a beautiful thing, even when those who use it say the ugliest things. There are a great many things wrong in this country, and many people lead difficult lives. People feel powerless in the face of bureaucracies, and goodness knows our current postmodernity is filled with frustrations. Our achy-breaky culture teaches us that uncivil responses are the most forceful kind, that respect blossoms in the barrel of a gun.

Rhetorical viciousness is perhaps the radio equivalent of violence, and the idea of talking trash in the face of an audience from the comfort and safety of one's own home certainly has its appeal for those who imagine themselves besieged by government and popular culture. In a muddied world, it's not surprising that some yearn to brush aside complications and subtleties —the "technicalities" of life, so to speak—in order to arrive at some kind of moral clarity. American life is teeming with figures who retail distilled worldviews; the great attraction of such "plain-spoken" gurus such as Rush Limbaugh, Ross Perot, Pat Robertson, and even Howard Stern is their gift for oversimplification. They are not the first to exploit the irrational, paranoiac symptoms of our national temper—their appeal is both primal and postliterate.

These demigods cast their little comedies with crude stereotypes and light their stages to emphasize the shadows. Cranking up the contrast, they attempt to drain away the gray.

What matters—and one suspects the talk show hosts would be the first to acknowledge this—are the voices of the callers. Even when the ideas expressed are, as often seems the case, simply the reheated opinions of a guru, the cast and pitch and modulation of the individual's voice matters on talk radio; for however long it is allowed to prattle on, that particular voice is The Show. In a way, these programs are little deconstructivist democracies, where every discreet thought is equivalent to every other. Each voice follows in its turn, berating its own demons, erecting its own idols.

All the hosts acknowledge that everyone has a right to his (or her) own opinion. Of course, most of the callers would reject the notion of equality—they are not relativists, they believe strongly in the meritocracy. Some ideas are more valid than others.

These call-in programs are like pornography. For a very small segment of the population, they provide a useful and necessary safety valve, an avenue for release of emotions that, if suppressed, might turn dangerous. For the rest of us, they offer only the cheapest, most tawdry kind of titillation. One can hardly blame decent people for being repulsed.

(1993)

TV: The Real World

A new cultural style has evolved, a mean ugliness that has poisoned the way we think about politics and government and life in general. In the Newt Age, civility is taken as a sign of weakness, as an indication of intellectual insecurity. We express ourselves in grunts and facile jabber, a nation under the influence of the talismanic power of advertising. We grab for bright and shiny things, unthinking brutes mesmerized by the tinkle of breaking glass.

Evidence of our sickness lies just ahead, on the back of the 1994 brown-over-tan Ford Explorer with a set of Ping golf clubs clacking against the rear glass. Two bumper stickers are affixed to this vehicle's tailgate. The first asks the alarming question "Where is Lee Harvey Oswald When We Need Him?" The second simply serves to advertise that the driver—a white male who looks to be about thirty-five years old, wearing a knit polo shirt, and, no doubt, Levi's Dockers jeans for the bigger-butted gentleman—votes "Pro-Life."

While the irony is wickedly delicious, and quite possibly intentional, one wonders what the proper response to such an outré display of cognitive dissonance and tastelessness ought to be. Maybe one should just go with the lumpy *zeitgeist* rising in one's throat, and jump from one's own car, pull the smug little jerk out of his $30,000 ride right in the middle of this quiet suburban street in this affluent neighborhood in the richest country on the planet and bash him into a coma with his own $200 custom-built, oversized, nine-degree-loft Big Bertha driver from Callaway Golf and stand over his cracked and moaning, soft-bellied bourgeois body and scream "Where is your mama when you need her, chum?" or "Where is your compassion and sense of social responsibility and decency?" until the police come and drag one away, howling and gnashing one's teeth.

Fits with the spirit of the season, doesn't it? These days, everyone is so crude, so drastic, so vulgar, so ready to go to war with their slogans and their fists. Just look at the new Gingrich GOP, fretting and strutting like Neon Deion Sanders sliding down the sidelines with an intercepted football and nothing but daylight ahead. These brave new politicos, who seize on grace or thoughtfulness as weakness, with them nothing is measured as they fight to win the week.

Isn't madness an appropriate response to a mad world? A world drunk on its own image, reflected and tempered through the glass of television?

•　　•　　•

All the wise people say television is evil, but that is hardly the point. Television is persistent, it simply *is*; it exists to sizzle violent in the corner of every true American home. It is the central tension in our lives; we struggle to use it as it struggles to use us—we want to be like the creatures that inhabit our artificial hearth.

And television, for its part, wants to sell us increasingly gaudy things. Bad merchandise, bad ideas, bad modes of thinking. It seeks to mold us into the kind of receptive consumers its sponsors require. We watch, hoping to find solace, amusement, the kind of tasty junk we might have grown out of had not the flickering machine robbed of us our attention spans. In this big country, television reduces everything to a containable size. It confers realness; nothing really seems real until it has acquired the sublime flatness of videotape. Then it becomes hyper-real, kissed with the authority of having been broadcast, of having been bounced off satellites, infused with a kind of sacredness. TV certifies stuff, makes it real.

We need to watch the Sophoclean drama of O. J. Simpson (or Tonya and Nancy) unfold on the small screen—television documents, provides us with an archive of common images with which to decorate our shabby, neglected souls. It gives us shrieking heads we can adopt as our own intellectual mascots. Television may be the enemy of thoughtfulness, but it is also unavoidable; as Dan Rather likes to remind us, the camera never blinks.

That's why they call the world within the tube *The Real World*. And the nineteen-inch Trinitron is just a window into it.

It is a realness we can all aspire to, for we are comfortable with television; these days we can all be on or at least act like we're on television. We've grown up with it; we've learned to assimilate the gestures and articulations of television celebrities. Television has rewired our cultural style; it has taught us to adopt the ironic detachment of artists like Warhol and Duchamp without dwelling on the accident of their work. We may not read so good, but we decode and deconstruct reflexively—one need not understand the anti-high seriousness polemics of Leslie Fielder and Susan Sontag to get the mild subversiveness of a David Letterman.

We are all ironic monsters now, adwise and street-smart. We know what messages we send and how to taunt and snarl like conquerors. We live stylized lives—lifestyles.

We should remember that television is almost always better at subverting seriousness than engaging in it. Gordon Van Sauter, the former CBS newsman who now heads the Fox News Division, coined the word "Foxonian" this year to describe that network's programming style, but the word might well be applied to the whole landscape ("wasteland," the pundits sniff) that is television.

So the self-referential, consciously trashy style of Fox programming is, in a sense, simply less hypocritical than the typical network sitcom. After all, the assumption is that we're all postmodern heroes here, able to slip the boundaries of suburban convention, equipped with an ironic stance that shields us from the contaminating influence of the salesmen on the other side of the glass.

At least that's the lie we tell ourselves, that we are in control, that we can always turn the fever off. The truth is, we've become Foxonian creatures, communicating in catch phrases and obscene gestures.

(1994)

An End to Prohibition

A Little Rock police officer was killed a few weeks ago; he was shot after he went through a suspected drug dealer's door.

There is not much the living can do for the dead but grieve and remember. Nor is there much we can supply a hero's family, aside from empty ceremony and death benefits. There aren't words soft enough to soothe the bereaved heart; all the well-meant homilies in the world are swallowed by fresh loss. We, the living, can only shake our heads at tragedy, then move on.

America is plagued by superstition. Our national superstition propelled that officer through that door and put the gun in the killer's hand. That officer went through that door because other officers had allegedly purchased rocks of crack cocaine there; after the shooting had stopped and the suspect had been shackled, they say they found a bit of marijuana in the apartment.

Our national superstition holds that drugs are something that cannot be tolerated by a good society and that drastic measures are necessary for their eradication. We are convinced that drugs are a criminal justice problem and that the only way to strike back at the epidemic is to send good brave men crashing through the doors of shoddy apartments in bad neighborhoods.

So we make war on drugs. We do so unthinkingly or after calculating the political cost of suggesting alternatives. In the last few years, we have decided to go after those who merely use drugs as well as those who profit from their sale. We have found that the drug trade won't be stifled by merely attacking the suppliers; the business is so lucrative that there is never any shortage of people willing to assume its terrible risks.

We continue the drug war because we imagine that abandoning it would be a kind of capitulation, a betrayal of those who've worked to remove drug dealers from our streets. But there are honorable alternatives to this bloody, senseless rite.

Perhaps the best alternative to the drug war would be a policy based on education and persuasion. During the last twenty-five years, a broad-based anti-tobacco campaign has convinced many millions of Americans that smoking cigarettes is unhealthy and dangerous. (That millions of people still smoke is a testament to either the addictive qualities of nicotine or the seductive powers of modern advertising.)

As the conservative columnist George Will has pointed out, drug misuse is not going away—we're either going to have a crime problem or a public health problem. And it makes more sense to not treat drug users as criminals. Just as we no longer toss alcoholics in drunk tanks, we should stop demonizing those who elect to get their kicks from substances other than nicotine, caffeine, and alcohol. All drugs are not necessarily dangerous, and self-medication, however ill-advised, does not necessarily constitute a crime.

At the same time, a responsible policy would recognize that—just as some people continue drinking to excess and smoking—there will be those who, despite the rational belief it is not good for them, will persist in using such hard drugs as cocaine and heroin. This is likely to be a rather small number, since although drug prosecutions do a poor job of rehabilitating drug misusers, treatment centers have about a 70 percent success rate. And putting a man in prison for a year is twice as expensive as treating him.

Moderation has followed legalization in the case of legal drugs; since the health boom of the 1970s, consumption of alcohol has declined as distilled spirits give way to wine coolers and light beer. During prohibition, alcohol had some of the same underground appeal that now attaches to heroin; with legalization came demystification and deglamorization that allowed most people to see alcohol for what it is—a social lubricant that, if used irresponsibly, can get you into a great deal of trouble.

It is unlikely a dramatic rise in drug consumption would follow legalization. Only 2 percent of Americans say they don't use drugs because drugs are illegal. What legalization would allow us to do is look at drugs realistically. While heroin—perhaps the most demonized of controlled substances—is highly addictive and deadly dangerous when taken in inexact and impure dosages, when taken over long periods of time it is physiologically more benign than heavy drinking or cigarettes. Criminalization is what drives addicts out of the world of work and respect, delivering them into the hands of unscrupulous, dangerous pushers.

Medically it seems to make little sense to force heroin addicts onto methadone, a drug that is superior to heroin only in that it can be legally prescribed. A rational drug policy would allow physicians to prescribe heroin as a painkiller—a use many pharmacologists think appropriate.

Marijuana is vastly less dangerous than heroin. There is strong evidence that the drug is useful in battling the nausea of chemotherapy and the effects of glaucoma and epilepsy. Other cannabis proponents make even stronger claims. Whatever the herb's therapeutic value, there is probably less harm in a joint of marijuana than in two fingers of Scotch.

Even cocaine and its street form, crack—a truly horrible substance—are, when seen in cold light, not nearly so evil as the warmongers paint them. Cocaine users do tend to use a lot of cocaine, not because it is physically addictive but because it is so pleasurable. Cocaine is not, as the folklore holds however, instantly addictive, if it is addictive at all. Legalization would immediately remove the profit motive from the cocaine trade, which even the most hawkish observer would admit is more dangerous than the drug itself. And crack, cocaine's cheapest and most insidious street form, exists only because of prices artificially inflated by prohibition.

Legalization is not a panacea, only an improvement. It wouldn't stop violent crime, merely eliminate its major cause. People would continue to misuse drugs. Addiction levels might even rise; yet the overall costs associated with drug use, direct and indirect, both to users and the rest of us, would certainly decrease.

The drug war is a perverse support system; without it, the illegal drug trade, which siphons off talented kids, would disappear. Poor people would no longer hide in their homes while dealers shoot it out in the street.

And good cops wouldn't die breaking through doors because the rest of us are afraid.

(1995)

95 •

Big Men
and Bell Curves

*"Civilization going to pieces," broke out Tom
violently. "I've gotten to be a terrible pessimist about
things. Have you read* The Rise of the Coloured
Empires *by this man Goddard?"*

"Why, no," I answered, rather surprised by his tone.

*"Well, it's a fine book and everybody ought to read
it. The idea is if we don't look out the white race will
be utterly submerged. It's all scientific stuff; it's been
proved."*

*"Tom's getting very profound," said Daisy with an
expression of unthoughtful sadness. "He reads deep
books with long words in them."*

—Scott Fitzgerald,
The Great Gatsby

In 1920, five years before Charles Scribners' Sons published
The Great Gatsby, they published a somewhat less enduring
work, a pseudoscientific treatise on the natural inferiority of
dark-skinned peoples called *The Rising Tide of Color,* by a man
named Lothrop Stoddard. It is instructive that Fitzgerald chose
to put this nasty book in the hands of his pious bully Tom—
surely no relation to Pat—Buchanan.

Racism is an indestructible component of American society;
it is an intractable problem of sufficient gravity to distort and
influence every aspect of social discourse and activity. It is not
an aberrant, curable condition which will someday pass into
anachronism; it is a sick but integral part of our national
character—like alcoholism, it can only be mitigated.

It is also interesting that, while Fitzgerald was not shy of
making use of contemporary phenomena in his novel (*Gatsby*

contains dozens of references to "real" people and events; he even alludes to a minor nineteenth-century Gothic romance, Maria Edgeworth's *Castle Rackrent*, which was obscure even in the 1920s), he chose to lightly disguise the Stoddard book.

We might suppose Scottie's tepid liberalism played a role in his electing not to lend credence or comfort to his fellow Scribner author; after all, people were as likely to misunderstand things in Scott's beloved Jazz Age as they are today, and the mention in *Gatsby* would surely have brought Stoddard's ideas to the attention of receptive readers. Even today, there are plenty of people who are susceptible to those kind of ideas—one hears rumors that Stoddard's book is being kept in print by one of those mail-order outfits that cater to white supremacists and irony junkies who find the whole business of hate-mongering amusing.

The idea that people different from "us," whoever "us" happens to be, are patently inferior, is an enduring and—truth be told—delicious conceit. Stoddard was not the first to claim that "lower races" threatened the cultural hegemony and standard of living of clean white people, nor even the most famous—in such people as Father Coughlin, Gerald L. K. Smith, and the post-KKK David Duke, there has always been a "respectable" face on white power.

William Shockley, the Nobel Prize–winning physicist, and Arthur Jensen, a Berkeley psychologist, came out with a fatuous study in 1969 which purported to demonstrate a relationship between race and performance on intelligence tests (as though the latter were indeed a reliable measure of "intelligence"). Shockley and Jensen were—surprise—of the opinion that blacks were less intelligent than whites and that genetics, not culturally biased tests nor economic deprivations, were primarily responsible.

A lot of people, most of them suffering from their own species of intellectual insecurity, are quick to believe in this claptrap. Even today, every so often amid the paranoiac talk radio cacophony, a voice will peep out to recommend that listeners "read Dr. Shockley's books." I heard one such voice a couple of weeks ago, even before the present firestorm, before a new presentation of the old "scientific" race theory, a book called *The Bell Curve*, took over the Op-Ed page of the *Wall Street Journal*, twenty-seven full pages in the *New Republic,* and the cover of *Newsweek.*

● ● ●

For those who haven't heard, *The Bell Curve* is an 850-page, statistics-laden argument for nature over nurture, and, only incidentally, for white supremacy. It says the same old thing, albeit with an apologist shamble. Its authors are a conservative ideologue named Charles Murray and a recently deceased Harvard psychologist, Richard Herrnstein. Murray's career was made by his 1984 book, *Losing Ground,* which provided a politically acceptable rationale for Reagan administration welfare cuts by arguing that anti-poverty programs actually hurt the poor by making them dependent on government help and thus lazy. This cruel, disingenuous theory that the poor are to blame for their own poverty has proved so politically alluring that it has, in the age of Bill Clinton, become a durable, bipartisan truism.

Murray and Herrnstein are careful to state that their "findings" ought to have no bearing on how individual whites and blacks view one another.

"We cannot think of a legitimate argument why . . . whites and blacks need be affected by the knowledge that an aggregate difference in measured intelligence is genetic rather than environmental," they write. So, having rendered the verdict that blacks are inherently inferior, that they—as a class—are less intelligent than whites, they blithely advise us that it doesn't really matter, since—oh joy—individual blacks can be just as smart as whites, maybe even smarter.

But if what they're saying is true, if there are significant differences in the cognitive abilities of the populations, then many of the fundamental assumptions about how Americans live are wrong. If blacks are less smart than whites—and if there is a relationship between low IQ and crime, poverty and dependence on government welfare programs—then it follows that blacks should have more difficulty overcoming these social pathologies. If blacks, as a group, possess inferior intellectual abilities, they become a drag on the social and economic progress of the nation, a second caste—the consequences of a "differently abled" black population are clear and chilling.

But what Murray and Herrnstein have submitted is not true and not helpful to the ongoing debate about how this country should approach problems of race and rights. Whatever "intelligence" may be, it is not something that can be reliably measured by testing—there are fabulously stupid people in Mensa, as well as bright illiterates scuffling homeless in the streets.

In a famous essay, Ralph Wiley allowed that he thought he was a fairly intelligent man until he took an IQ test in Martinique.

And the idea of "race" is nearly as occluded as that of "intelligence"; there are greater intraracial differences between, say, "black men" than between "black men" and "white men." Despite the insistence of Murray and Herrnstein in drawing lines, most of the current science is leaning toward the construct that people are people—environmental and cultural factors account for our differences.

Still, there is a debate about that. In the angry, balkanized America we nowadays inhabit, we have developed ways of dismissing each other and obliterating argument. We freely avail ourselves of the exterminating gesture—we call names: "liberal," "fascist," "racist." It would be easy to dismiss *The Bell Curve* simply on the basis of its inconvenient premise. It would be easy to brand Murray and Herrnstein "racist," but less useful than showing that they are wrong.

Books get written and written about for all kinds of reasons, but the most important reason usually has to do with the author's self-interest. People will say all kinds of things in books to try to sell them; there is even that Havard Ph.D., Nack or somebody, who "believes" in UFOs. This trashy pseudoscience gets marketed because America is filled with Tom Buchanans, all looking for deep books with long words to make them feel like Supermen.

(1994)

Having MTV

While MTV doesn't get—and maybe doesn't deserve—much respect from adults, it's never been as bad as all that.

It's not really cutting-edge; it's not really dangerous; it's not really even very hip. What it is is a utility, a money pump for the corporate culture that uses it to get inside the pockets of those elusive and desirable fourteen- to thirty-four-year-old consumers. It's not a very complicated idea, just a successful one.

Even people who never watch MTV are conversant with its conventions and images. MTV has literally changed the way we *look* at pop music; it has exploited the abbreviated attention spans of a people raised before an electronic hearth, and it has supplied us with a national iconography, a gallery of leather-strapped heroes and villains who prance and buck across the collective imagination. We are surrounded by the creatures of MTV—little Princes and Madonnas and thug-lite gangstas roam our shopping malls and grammar schools; grown men wear sunglasses they noticed in a Don Henley video.

And, as radio programming has become increasingly balkanized, with stations increasingly selling themselves on the basis of what they won't play ("no rap, no heavy metal, no country, no dance divas with the whispering voices of fashion models"), MTV has become the arbiter of pop stardom. Top Forty radio no longer exists, but MTV is there to supply us with a consensus hoard of riffs and images. With its images of impossibly sexy women and incipiently violent, sullen men, MTV is there for anyone to demonize. It plays the "beast" well, with its glib-yet-inarticulate video jockeys, its *laissez-faire* attitude about sex, and its feigned hostility to white men in blue suits, to those who in another age and time would have been called "squares." MTV has cut out its own corner of the culture, a time and space continuum that bears no resemblance to the real world (instead, it thrusts strangers together in a video-surveilled ant farm and calls that *The Real World*), where social reality and cultural history dare not intrude. MTV makes noise, loud noise that bleeds over into the lives of even those who would ignore it. MTV plays politics and gets the attention of Bill Clinton and Al Gore and even—pathetically, too late—George Bush, who met the fresh-scrubbed Tabitha Soren on the caboose of his campaign train after it was clear he could not win. MTV is not all bad and not all good. MTV is America; we must pay attention.

MTV shapes culture, is culture—a grinding, devouring sales tool. It must valorize consumerism and celebrate capitalism, even as it seems to embody attitudes and values diametrically opposed to the interests of its corporate masters. MTV is intriguing—and important—because it is rooted in the culture of rock 'n' roll, a culture of rebellion (or at least of the unregenerative pose)—rebellion it is designed to package and sell. It has a considerable stake in preserving the status quo. It is run by those white guys in blue suits.

"The corporate world," Bob Dylan said a few years ago, "when they figured out what (rock) was and how to use it, they snuffed the breath out of it and killed it. Used to be, they were afraid. You know, like 'hide your daughters,' . . . Elvis, Little Richard, Chuck Berry, they struck fear in their hearts. Now they got a purpose, to sell soap, bluejeans, Kentucky Fried Chicken, whatever . . . it's all been neutralized, nothing threatening, nothing magical, nothing challenging. I hate to see it, because you know it set me free, set the whole world on fire . . . There's a lot of us who still remember."

And a lot of us who can't. A whole generation has been raised up in its flickering wash of color and deceit. It was at exactly one minute past midnight on August 1, 1981, when a band called The Buggles—a band that would be forgotten if not for their historic age—issued in a new pop age with a prophetic, synth-soaked song called "Video Killed the Radio Star." At first the new network's playlist was incredibly thin; MTV started with a library of only 250 clips, 30 of which featured Rod Stewart.

At first it was all videos, introduced by one of five bland and unknown "VJs." MTV's obvious model was the sports network ESPN—the idea was to target a desirable demographic by broadcasting promotional music clips produced by record companies. It worked. Originally available to only 2.5 million subscribers,

MTV cost Warner Brothers a modest $30 million to start. Within two years, it was the highest-rated cable channel (it still is); by 1984 it was making money.

And not just for its corporate masters; MTV also boosted a slumping music industry (it didn't take the record companies long to realize that the production of video clips was indeed a cost-effective means of promoting not only a record, but an artist and even a whole pop genre), and the flashy, quick-edit techniques used by video directors soon drove changes in fashion, TV, and publishing. MTV altered the way the public looked at rock bands; untelegenic or video-resistant groups found themselves overshadowed by under-talented "haircut" bands such as Duran Duran.

While a performer's image and appearance had always been important—it wasn't musicality or creativity that separated Elvis from Carl Perkins or Roy Orbison—MTV made it necessary for all aspiring rock stars to understand and adapt to the aesthetic requirements of video stardom. (One of the most popular videos of 1995—actually No. 11 on MTV's Top 100 Video Countdown— played against audience expectations in the video age. In "Run-Around," a clip promoting a song by the rootsy band Blues Traveler, the real band is hidden behind an Oz-like curtain and glimpsed only briefly while a faux group made up of attractive types cavorts on stage for public consumption.) While most of the early videos consisted of concert footage or of the band lip-syncing the song (often in an incongruous setting), video directors (and artists and record companies) soon grew more ambitious, less tentative.

Some artists didn't even appear in their own clips, while others—most notably aging Boston rockers Aerosmith—were content to assume supporting roles while actors played out the story lines of their songs. According to Mick Jagger's dictum, rock 'n' roll has always been more about the singer than the song; the video-making process, by mingling visual riffs and hooks with the musical, intensifies this confusion of performer and performance. Madonna's videos, no matter who actually creates them, seem an extension of her personality and to a large extent are inseparable from her stardom. Videos become a performer's persona—not even Madonna is Madonna when she's not being amplified by television.

MTV is a mythic construct, and the performers (and the VJs) who appear on MTV are servants to that construct. The purpose of that construct is to sell us jeans and compact discs and serious video-game equipment.

And that's not all bad. Looking at MTV these days, it's difficult to believe that, up until 1983, it maintained a lily-white play list. Michael Jackson, with the awesome backing of Columbia Records, was the video Jackie Robinson, crashing the color line with unassailable verve and talent. "Billie Jean" is still one of the most recognizable, most potent cultural artifacts of the decade. For a while, the channel still seemed dominated by heavy metal headbangers, but after Jackson the influx of black artists was inevitable. Even rap began showing up on the channel, first ghetto-ized into half-hour blocks, later dropped into regular heavy rotation. MTV is perhaps the most important factor in the darkening of the pop charts—these days "black pop" seems a strained distinction—arguably the most popular group in America is TLC, a trio of black women who blend soulful R&B with elements of jazz and hip hop. The most popular video in the country in 1995 was "Gangsta's Paradise" by a thirty-year-old black man from California who calls himself Coolio.

Indeed, a random half-hour of MTV on New Year's Day yielded the following: "Ruby SoHo" by an Oakland band called Rancid, sporting the dyed Mohawks and thick accents of late-seventies British punk bands, followed by two video versions of a hip-hop ballad ("California Love") by 2Pac "featuring" Dr. Dre, followed by a wimpy guitar pop song called "Breakfast at Tiffany's" by the folk-rock band Deep Blue Something. Then some commercials. Then LL Cool J and the vocal group Boyz II Men combining on a croony rap hybrid called "Hey Lover," followed by "The World I Know," a grungy tune from Collective Soul, and finally Madonna's creamy ballad "You'll See." And then, of course, more commercials.

However slow MTV was to embrace black artists, it is clear the channel is now one of music's least segregated neighborhoods. While it is folly to believe MTV a meritocracy, there are few places in America's culture where questions of ethnicity seem so irrelevant. There is a kind of nervy "United Colors of Benetton" quality that pervades MTV's programming—even the game show *Singled Out* (a kind of updated dating game) is delightfully oblivious to questions of race. This would seem to be a hopeful sign, since MTV is—despite its posturing—decidedly not cutting-edge. It is flip, juvenile, and irreverent, but fiscally conservative. The new bands that get airplay on MTV are the bands that have already secured the backing of an established record company.

And while MTV's news programming affects a sleekly liberal patina, the most vigorous political voice on the network is that of the VJ Kennedy—the fun-loving conservative chick with the hots for Rush Limbaugh. And MTV was quick to create a second channel—the milquetoasty VH-1—for those hipness-impaired viewers who couldn't deal with the angst and anger of the regular rotation. (And, while VH-1 may not play Rancid or Bushwick Bill, you can bet MTV plays the soothing pop of Mariah Carey and Hootie & the Blowfish.)

But it is as hard to argue that MTV has had a detrimental effect on rock 'n' roll as it is to argue that MTV is what it pretends to be—a hip venue for cutting-edge music for connoisseurs. MTV is cynical, as almost all pop music is cynical. It is shifty and contradictory, just like the rest of pop culture. To raise the issue of co-optation is to miss the point—rock has always been a commodity, available to whomever wants to exploit it. The 4/4 beat belongs to no one, and to everyone; it's neither moral nor immoral (though the White Citizens' Committees and professionally virtuous opportunists like Michael Medved will always argue differently). A laughably misguided advertising campaign in the 1960s held that "The Man Can't Bust Our Music." Well, maybe not—but The Man can try to control it and to bend it to his purposes.

You want your MTV? Well, you can have it—for a price.

(1996)

What Were
the Police Doing
in the Park?

Two obvious questions present themselves in the wake of the arrest of a Little Rock television weatherman in a North Little Rock park early this year:

First we must consider what the weatherman was doing in the park between newscasts on a Monday evening. According to police, he was "looking for a good time." According to the police, he acted in a lewd manner. According to the weatherman, he did no such thing. He was arrested on a charge of public sexual indecency—a misdemeanor—and taken to the local jail. He posted bond and was released. The next morning his attorney phoned in a "not guilty" plea to the court.

Now it is obvious that our society does not consider the crime the weatherman is accused of committing a very serious offense. One does not allow, say the Unibomber, to phone in his pleas. Indeed, most of these public sexual indecency cases seem to be disposed of without much fuss; sometimes the names of those arrested end up in the newspaper, sometimes they don't. "Public sexual indecency" may sound like a sordid and unhappy offense, but it isn't robbery or murder or even grand theft auto. It's not the sort of thing they built *Dragnet* episodes around.

All right then, to answer the first question: Either the weatherman was in the park in search of a sexual adventure, or he was talking a walk to clear his head. We can't know, we can only speculate. On an afternoon radio talk show, it was suggested—by callers and even the host himself—that perhaps this wasn't the first time the weatherman had been to a local park and encountered undercover policemen. In this newsroom—and probably in most other workplaces around the state—prurient interests were aroused. We all had our little feast of *Schadenfreude*.

Now, we all should be ashamed of ourselves for enjoying the pain suffered by another. Yet the weatherman cannot complain too loudly. He became a public person voluntarily and has pursued a career wherein his celebrity is itself an asset. He is a big boy; he knows what risks accrue. Even if he is not guilty he is not so innocent as to not know why some men take to the parks at dusk. It is an ugly thing to enjoy his embarrassment, but none of those who smirked and tittered put the weatherman on that path. He has much to explain, but not to us. He has to explain to his family, to his friends, to those who might have been disappointed by his being where he was when he was. Whatever he was doing in the park, it is no business of yours and mine.

•   •   •

And now on to the second, greater question:

What were the police doing in that park?

Well, they tell us they were detailed to clean it up, but we know that they are there to harass homosexuals. Gay men come to the park to meet other gay men and have a genital sneeze. That is not a healthy way to live, it is not safe, and it is not the kind of life any of us would wish upon our loved ones. But it is what happens.

Gay men gather in our parks at dusk because our society is yet so homophobic as to squeeze them into the margins. We make outlaws of homosexuals; we deny them the dignity of living openly, of courting openly. We make them ashamed of themselves, and we drive them to assuming risks that only the self-loathing could accept.

We drive them into the parks at dusk, and then we send in undercover policemen who wear tight jeans and pose for them. These policemen coo and flirt and then arrest the sad and lonely men who take their bait.

It is a perverse practice, a waste of time and precious police resources, but they go into the park and walk the trails and look for the desperate men who cruise. They make eye contact. They work the parks.

I hope the policemen who have to work the trails are ashamed of themselves. I hope they go home feeling dirty—not because their duty has brought them into the proximity of people who love a different way from most of us, but because what they are doing is wrong and sick, beneath any human being's dignity. Better to scoop out the kennels with your bare hands, officer, than to do this kind of work.

That is not to say that we should allow libertine behavior in the parks. We should not. We should not allow people to drink and litter or blow a little dope down there, either. Maybe we need a police presence in the park but why undercover officers? Why not wear the uniform, the hat, the gun, the whole nine yards?

Tell you what, you catch a weatherman in the park with a police officer in uniform, then you can try to ruin his life.

Why not deter rather than entrap? Who needs to see arrest figures—body counts—that bad? Does our city need the money from fines, the heap of wrecked lives, that badly?

It is a good scam. Most people will go quietly. The fine is not so large—$250 or so—and most people, whether they believe they have been entrapped or not, pay the fine with a whimper and promise not to go back to the park.

OK, so this state has a sodomy law. So what?

It is a stupid, unjust, barbaric law. And most people know that. Most of the members of the General Assembly know it, though only two have seen fit to publicly voice their opposition.

Gays, lesbians, and bisexuals are with us, and like the poor they will be with us always. The state ought have nothing to say about what two consenting adults choose to do with each other's bodies. What people do in private ought to remain private.

And what they do in public parks might be a matter for the police—if we could be sure that the police aren't the precipitating factor. Catch a weatherman in the park soliciting a police officer in full drag, hey, I think we can agree that that weatherman needs to be soundly censured.

So what were the police doing in the park? Nothing any good. They were preying on the weak and susceptible; like common muggers, like low-grade extortionists, they were after the easy mark. And that *is* our business, and we all ought be ashamed.

(1996)

The Yankee Woman

On the flight home from Cleveland I sat next to a Yankee woman who wanted to talk.

Before I go any further I should explain that I am not the kind of southerner who habitually uses "Yankee" as an adjective. Indeed, while I am most definitely a southerner (Savannah-born like my mother; my father came from Asheville, I still say "ma'am" and sometimes my voice softens into a legitimate drawl), I'm not the kind of southerner who often refers to himself as a "Southerner." I feel no need to remind the less fortunate of their disadvantages.

It should be apparent that I bear the Yankee no ill will, that I am not preoccupied with the old grievance. I am ready to forgive if not forget (forgetting would be sinful). After all, I married a Yankee girl; had I not, there would have been no reason for me to even be on that flight from Cleveland. We were up there attending to her folks.

Anyway, by referring to this lady as a "Yankee woman" I am telling you something about her and something else about myself.

First of all, you may surmise that she was, well, direct. And that she had no qualms about engaging a stranger—even a stranger holding on his lap a dog-eared paperback copy of *The Last Gentleman*—in what passed for conversation. She was quite forward, this lady.

Not that she wasn't nice. She was perfectly nice, if a bit insensitive to her neighbor's preference for Walker Percy over news of alien nephews and ex-husbands and lawsuits to be settled or pursued. To be fair, she had a moderately interesting biography, though probably not interesting enough to discuss in much detail here. Anyway, that's what the adjective "Yankee" should tell you about that lady. And here's what my use of that adjective should tell you about me:

That while I would rather spend an hour feigning interest— nodding and smiling and uh-huh-ing and is-that-so-ing—than risk offending a stranger, I eventually strike back. I even up the accounts, I turn my hour of discomfiture into a little newspaper fable. That's how it works: the Yankee woman annoys me, and I never let on that I am annoyed. Then I come back to the safety of my desk, and, taking cover behind piles of books and stacks of paper, I return fire.

You must beware of me, Yankee Woman. I'll smile and nod at your little domestic homilies and horror stories, but when you're out of sight and have forgotten you ever distracted me, I'll draw my sniper's bead on you. Ping.

Such is the prerogative of us conquered folk—we assume guerrilla ways.

•   •   •

I doubt I would have spent any time at all thinking about the Yankee woman had she not offended me. She didn't offend me by bothering me. That is, I know, my fault. I could have turned into my book and ignored her, or pretended sleepiness or more politely put her off (although I don't know how, I'm sure I've seen it done). That she did not sense my discomfort proves my southerness.

No, she offended me by one of the stories she told me about herself. I will give you the abridged version:

Because of her husband's job, she, some years ago, found herself living in the South, an experience she said she found unpleasant (no wonder; though she knew I was getting off at Little Rock, she never guessed I was a southerner). One morning she saw a young woman on television speaking with a southern drawl and she was offended.

"She kept saying 'you-all,'" the Yankee woman told me. "She couldn't speak correctly. And this was a show that children could watch. You can't have children saying 'you-all'—you get out in the real world and say 'you-all' and everybody is going to think you're a dummy."

The Yankee woman was distressed by this newscaster—and after agonizing about it for a few days, she decided to do something about it. She called the station manager and asked if he had "ever listened to" this particular newscaster.

Why, yes, ma'am, he had.

And he hadn't noticed anything funny about her speech? Why, no, ma'am, he had not.

Well, maybe he should pay a little closer attention. After all, the newscaster just could not speak correctly.

A week later, the newscaster was gone. And though the Yankee woman felt a little bad about that, well, it was just something she felt she had to do.

• • •

Now you and I know that the Yankee woman had nothing to do with getting the newscaster fired or demoted. You and I know that that station manager probably just shook his weary head and that the newscaster probably got a better job, moved to New York, and changed her name to Diane Sawyer. Or something like that.

Now my accent comes and goes, and some people believe I lost it long ago. I will admit it seems to return at opportune times, when I wish to impress the fact of my regionality upon an audience. When I was working in Phoenix there was a gentleman, originally from Virginia I believe, whom we often had to call to ask for comment on one story or another. Over the years, this gentleman had become convinced—as gentlemen sometimes do—that the best way to deal with any inquiry from my newspaper was a terse "no comment." In fact, most of the time he wouldn't even come to the phone.

Of course, in this business, you never fail to call the gentleman to ask for a comment—even if you know that no comment will be forthcoming. As fate would have it, soon after arriving in Phoenix I wrote a story that required me to call this gentleman.

No comment, his secretary said.

Why?

Because he doesn't trust your newspaper.

Would the gentleman be so good as to tell me that himself?

Wait—the secretary said—I'll ask.

He came to the phone and told me just that. Suddenly I was a courtly Georgian. I thanked him for showing me the proper courtesy. And I did not press him to say anything; I accepted his no comment. And the next time I called him, he did respond to my questions. And he answered my questions the time after that and the time after that.

It is a measure of her Yankeeness that the woman on the plane genuinely believes she got that poor newscaster fired, just as surely as she believes "you-all" is an abomination.

It is a measure of my southerness that I feel just a little bit bad about making her look silly. But there is an advantage in being underestimated. And speaking "correctly" ain't everything, ma'am.

(1996)

Toward a Tyranny
of the Dull Normal

Offending the Audience, a 1966 play by Peter Handke, locates the uses of outrage as well as anything I've ever come across: "We will offend you because offending you is also one way of speaking to you. . . . While we are offending you, you won't just hear us, you will listen to us. The distance between us will no longer be infinite. . . . We will only create an acoustic pattern. . . . Since you are probably offended already, we will waste no more time before throughly offending you, you chuckleheads."

This is the Giddy Age, a time when silly people such as North Carolina senator Jesse Helms and California representative Dana Rohrabacher have succeeded in making ordinary naughtiness seem profound and dangerous. To watch the mud-wrestling matches between the "moralists" and the academic apologists might be good clean sport—were not serious questions about the way we conduct our lives at stake. Though shock as an aesthetic tactic became passé about twenty years ago, we chuckleheads have lately been engaged in a debate over the cultural legitimacy of puerility and the audio-visual depiction of nasty sex. "Me So Horny," the call-and-response ditty by the notorious Miami rap group 2 Live Crew, seems of the same cloth as the unindicted nursery rhymes of Andrew Dice Clay and scatological childhood chants. As a nation we seem suddenly amazed as we contemplate that region below our navels. We blush, snigger, and call for the authorities. What the hell is going on?

In the 1980s, the first years of The Plague and the reign of Rap Master Ron, the American impulse was to retreat from the libertine attitudes of the sixties and seventies. It was the age of the moral majority, of televangelism and a new cold morning in America. AIDS hit, and some fundamentalists grew grim smiles as they mused at how retribution inevitably follows illicit behavior. Low art, at least, imitates life—not the other way around—and the result was Glenn Close as an avenging hussy in *Fatal Attraction,* Dr. Ruth's clinical stand-up routines, George Michael's monogamy rap, and the general retro-fitting of our national psyche. Sexual outlawism had always been dangerous, but now it was deadly and a new cult of "innocence" emerged. Call it repression if you will, but during the last part of the decade it seemed as if the surgeon general had decreed that any representation of sex outside of marriage must carry a warning label—when Robert Chambers murdered Jennifer Levin the *New York Post* blared "Rough Sex Killed Jenny?"

Michael Jackson, an asexual and untouchable creature, was a suitable pop idol of the 1980s, where synthetic sweetness and otherworldly weirdness played better than orthodox sexual ardor. Jackson is a fantasy being, divorced from messy carnality and suspended in a chilly, self-constructed image cocoon. He provided the safest sex of all, a mild, prepubescent tingle of mysterious longing.

Like Jackson, today's primary pop icon, Madonna, has erased the line between performance and persona. She is the Iron Slut, a sex kitten who finds herself none the dumber for having skipped college. Madonna is the one pervasive figure who seems in control of both libido and market, rehabilitating Marilyn Monroe while enforcing her own strict, neo-Wagnerian code of excellence. She knows every riff of American womanliness from butch to femme, from Scarlet (Hester and O'Hara) to Josephine Baker to Sally Field as Sister Bertrille (why not?) and plays each one well. "Play" is the operative word, like Deborah Harry (the last great pop white girl, devoured by Reaganism), Madonna is at once both a critic of femininity and its high priestess; her coy "affair" with comedian/singer Sandra Bernhard (a pop heroine in her own right) was a deft media put-on, teased around like two chicks at a slumber party before finally denying any potential carnal aspect of their relationship.

Yet despite Madonna's smarts—she has become a critic's darling, no mean feat for a thin-voiced bleach blonde whose music is derivative and absolutely incidental to her *schtick*—the general perception (a perception she in fact encourages) is of a talentless bimbo gamming her ruthless way to the top. Madonna assumes she will be misunderstood; that is part of the act—she enlists the chuckleheads in her performance—witness the mid-1980s "wannabes," a term which has passed into the lexicon but was coined to describe little Madonna clones. While "Material Girl" was a spoof on the Marilyn mystique, to some it seemed like Eddie Murphy's worst nightmare given voice. Her record "Justify My Love" is a slight affair that recalls Donna Summer and Diana Ross and pre-AIDS libidinous ardor, but her most important recent project was a public service announcement designed to encourage young people to vote that aired on MTV during the election season. Bedecked in Old Glory, Madonna swirled, vogued, and reminded us that "Freedom of speech is better than sex . . ." At the end of the bit she parted the flag and revealed her Nautilized body, clad in a red, white, and blue bikini.

As a bit of choreography, it owed more than a little to the final vignette in Nicholas Roeg's powerful film version of Bernhard's one-woman Broadway show, *Without You I'm Nothing*, which left us with Bernhard wearing nothing but the world's smallest, flag-colored G-string and star-shaped pasties dancing to Prince's sex paean "Little Red Corvette." The film also includes a brief, hilarious bit with a Madonna impersonator and a mid-film pan over Bernhard's bed, where she is ferociously copulating with a sculpted black man—a Mapplethorpian tableau.

Bernhard and Madonna are smart women, alert to the political possibilities—sexual and otherwise—of their respective dirty dances. This isn't the pent-up 1980s anymore, these patriots announced, but not all sexual adventurers are as keen as these two, and even if they were, a substantial demographic element absorbs it all as mere self-display, designed primarily to incite titillation.

"Tamed as it may be," Susan Sontag wrote in her 1967 essay "The Pornographic Imagination," "sexuality remains one of the demonic forces in human consciousness—pushing us at intervals to taboo and dangerous desires, which range from impulse to commit sudden arbitrary violence upon another person to the voluptuous yearning for the extinction of one's consciousness, for death itself." Perhaps 1980s repressionism is as responsible for the emergence of rough rap as the much-trotted-out black oral tradition of signifying, the theory Prof. Henry Louis Gates Jr. used in his courtroom deconstruction of 2 Live Crew. (The good professor did not, however, equate the Crew with

Shakespeare, despite what you may have read in the mongering press.) But if the Crew are nasty, then what of Houston's Geto Boys? In "Mind of a Lunatic" the rappers graphically depict the Mansonesque rape and murder of a woman:

She begged me not to kill her—I gave her a rose
Then I slit her throat, watched her shake till her eyes closed
Had sex with her corspe before I left her
And drew my name on the wall like Helter Skelter

Though Geffen Records has refused to release the Geto Boys' album because they judge it overly violent, sexist, racist, and—their term—indecent, the question seems less whether the record should be released (since pop culture is marketing, if there is a paying audience out there—and there is—the product will find its way out) but why such music is being made in the first place. In the wake of 2 Live Crew's recent legal vindication, Luther Campbell looked into the cameras and tape recorders and asked, "Don't you like bitches? I like bitches," and proceeded to assert his support of the First Amendment.

Needless to say, the First Amendment deserves less trivial champions than these rough rappers. Though a lot of people might like them to, only a fascist would force them to shut up. And, presumably, only a cretin would want to pay money to hear them.

But maybe we're a nation of cretins. The aforementioned Dice Clay has his devotees, and 2 Live Crew ships platinum (they ought cut their prosecutors in on the royalties). People read Jackie Collins, for heaven's sake. We are stuck with a permanent underculture of the literal minded (who would argue that the Geto Boys "celebrate" murder and rape and seek to suppress them) and the developmentally arrested (who keep copies of *Hustler* in their credenzas and giggle at sitcom double entendres).

That is our burden—our Republic must accommodate all sorts of vulgar mindedness. It is almost as barbarous to suggest that Robert Mapplethorpe is much more than a competent commercial photographer who enjoyed a certain chic among magazine editors and celebrities as it is to brand him a pornographer. Mapplethorpe's defiant homosexuality—especially after he has

been expunged by AIDS—is perhaps what really tweaks his enemies. In his "XYZ Portfolios" there are a few images of unregenerate sado-masochism—including the infamous bullwhip
photo—but his nudes of children are almost cloying and only a
sick or disingenuous mind could, as Pat Robertson did, call them
"kiddie porn."

The question of whether they should be hanging in a gallery
is a close one—but it is one for museum curators and directors
to decide, not the state. Any reasonable adult knows this, but as
any reasonable adult also knows, we are not surrounded by reasonable adults. Jesse Helms's and others' political showman-
ship has made us a nation of critics—some of us willing to
deliver judgments without ever having experienced the work
in question. While Helms may be one of the few people to
interpret Mapplethorpe's art the way the artist intended—
that Mapplethorpe intended his photographs to be subversive
is clear, even if they resemble nothing so much as perfume
advertisements—the senator's reaction to the photographer's
love taps against the empire is reactionary and childish. How
seriously can you take a man who, in the Senate chamber, asked
all the women and the adolescent pages to leave, so he could
display the "disgusting" Mapplethorpe photographs to the concerned menfolk?

The answer of course is that we had better take Helms very
seriously. Even if he is a big baby, he has a constituency that
ranges far beyond North Carolina and an agenda that ranges far
beyond those artists (if any) who are supported by the National
Endowment of the Arts. Helms knows how to connect with a
postliterate, homophobic, scared-to-death-of-minorities crowd
—show 'em pictures and feed them back their fears. That's what
they did with Willie Horton and what they've tried to do with 2
Live Crew. Renegade black male sexuality—miscegenation and
the Mandingo complex—and its attendant myths and mysteries
is at the core of America's racial misery.

It doesn't much matter that 2 Live Crew's audience is
mixed—they attract as many straight white male fans as any
other rap group, a lot more than, say, Public Enemy—what matters is that the performers are young black men. It scares us, it
titillates us, and if we're honest we know deep down that it's

why half the country wants to ban them while the other half knows all the words to "Dick Almighty."

Dumb testosterone rage, of course, is not the exclusive province of rough rap groups like 2 Live Crew, Ice Cube, and the Geto Boys. Misogyny and the objectification of young women are time-honored rock 'n' roll (the name itself is a euphemism for sex) tradition, with the girl-baiting of the Rolling Stones perhaps the archetypal example. While the fundamentalist/guerrilla feminist premise is that pornography has created the current appetite for the puerile, that view is both simplistic and wrongheaded. Porn, after all, is a slippery, fluid thing that exists primarily in the tender mind of the fetishist, and the documented decay of the American attention span requires an escalation of vividness and explicitness. Spectacle becomes essential—whether it is made apparent in the rising body counts of Stallone/ Schwarzenegger movies or intensified sexual explicitness in music, film, and visual art.

The most frightening cultural event witnessed this year was the Dice Clay vehicle, *The Adventures of Ford Fairlane.* Not because it was sexist, racist, or obscene, but because it was aimed at such a mindless, callow, insecure sensibility; it was because someone's market research found evidence of a potential audience for the film (happily, it was not a hit, though when we saw it the theaters were full and raucous).

As rock, an intentionally juvenile music, has become the dominant agent in pop culture (to the point where it subsumes literary pretenders like Bret Easton Ellis and sports figures like tennis punk Andre Agassi and football casualty Brian "Bozworth"), the juvenile aesthetic has become the primary way of looking at accessible art. An image has got to kick ass before it registers with the unsubtle, calloused minds of the American swarm. At the broadest end of the brush—television, radio, rock, and mass-market film—we are dangerously close to a tyranny of the dull normal.

(1990)

A Serious Lack
of Seriousness

If these essays can be said to have a theme—and I'm not at all sure that they can, or, for that matter, that having a theme is necessarily preferable to wandering around kicking over rocks—it might be a minor obsession with the American way of frivolity, a way of being that I have occasionally called the American Frolic.

This "American Frolic" is essentially a lack of seriousness in dealing with the critical moral choices facing us as a nation and as individuals. It seems that Americans have been conditioned to react, not to consider. We are very good at ripostes and snappy comebacks, at cracking wise and looking smart, but we fail to genuinely engage most of the issues with which we pretend to be most concerned.

Trained by television and "the media"—one of those amorphous, vaguely technical-sounding words of scant meaning that our culture so cherishes—we all gesticulate with flair and most of us can yap very well, employing all manner of slick rhetorical devices and obliterating gestures. We elect our intellectual mascots—a Rush Limbaugh, a Louis Farrakhan, a Ross Perot, a Thomas Sowell, an Ayn Rand, a Jean Houston or Anthony Robbins—to do our thinking for us; we are a nation divided into rooting interests. We sign up as members of a thought tribe in lieu of genuinely thinking.

We continually talk past one another, resorting to cant and partisan boilerplate. We adopt dubious argumentative tactics; as every talk radio host knows, it's not very difficult to win an argument when you get to make up both sides.

Seriousness is so rare that we are considered foolish to expect it. No serious person would contend—as has been contended by people in serious-looking clothes—that people in Arkansas pay more taxes than people in other states. It just isn't true—though it is certainly possible to make the argument that people in Arkansas are overtaxed.

When a police chief defends his department from a news-paper columnist's "attacks" not by addressing the columnist's questions but by accusing the columnist of consorting with the American Civil Liberties Union—a crime in the eyes of most of those who haven't elected the ACLU their particular intellectual mascot—that police chief is not being serious. There are very real questions—I don't assume the answer is clear-cut—about whether secret police are any more effective in keeping nuisances out of our public parks than uniformed officers in marked vehicles, or, for that matter, whether we ought allow police to work "undercover" in order to sniff out drug dealers. A serious society would recognize there are real questions about whether we ought to be treating this country's drug problems as a criminal matter at all.

A serious society would recognize that what political operatives call "spin" is simply a variety of lies, that the manufacture of scandal is a lucrative business, that it is in the interest of some to convince the rest of us that the country is in a perpetual state of crisis. Yet we remain wide-eyed and credulous whenever the spinner or alarmist happens to subscribe to the same set of magazines as we do. We live in a world infested by prophets of certainty—men and women who will tell you they know for a fact that things are this way or that way and, given these circumstances, this is how we ought to behave.

A serious society would understand and accept that there are things that are unknowable and that certainty is a refuge for those who, for whatever reason, cannot accept the mystery that lingers in the world. If all you want is answers, there are plenty of people who'll sell them to you.

All I know is that those people who pretend to know don't know. They are guessing, just like the rest of us.

• • •

Now, when I use the word "seriousness" I do not mean "joy-lessness" or "grumpiness." My definition of seriousness simply requires treating ideas with respect and considering the consequences of our decisions. It means listening to, and considering, the opinions of those whose experiences and philosophies do not coincide with our own.

The late Prof. Allan Bloom, a man with whom one can find much to disagree, once wrote that "a serious life means being fully aware of the alternatives, thinking about them with all the intensity one brings to bear on life-or-death questions in full recognition that every choice is a great risk with necessary consequences that are hard to bear."

Real choices are only available to those who face real questions. And the real questions aren't about brand-loyalty politics or whether one is a rocker or a punk but about how one chooses to conduct and furnish one's life.

Seriousness charges us with thinking about the Big Things, with considering what might happen if our choices turn out to be wrong (or right). Seriousness also requires that we perform a kind of intellectual triage—for instance, a Bible study group ought to have better things to discuss than whether the current president has ever cheated on his wife.

If we were serious, we would be able to find ways to talk about such seemingly intractable problems as abortion, capital punishment, and drugs. We would refuse to be distracted by non-issues such as flag burning. We could begin to see that "issues" such as "character" and "family values" aren't issues in the true sense of the term—no one argues for bad character or immorality, such buzzwords are simply convenient labels to affix to those we don't like or feel we can't agree with—and that the real issue in this country is probably something so dry as the enduring American debate over the limits of federalism.

We ought to be concerned that many high school students in this country have neither the interest nor the ability to read a book for pleasure. We ought to be concerned that people are suffering and that our cities are collapsing, that our culture has been debased to the point that we honk like geese at silly sitcoms and mistake bullies and loudmouths for heroes and leaders.

(1996)

• *reports* •

Halloween

We all heard the story, and we believed it, whether it was true or not.

Two boys, about our age, maybe a grade ahead or a grade behind us, were teasing the old man, ringing his doorbell and running off. The old man couldn't move around very well, he couldn't chase them, and even if he caught them he didn't know their names or where they lived. He was an old man, and they were just neighborhood kids, with English Racers and P. F. Flyers.

They had kept it up for weeks, and the game had always worked the same way. From the safety of the bushes around the corner of the house, they could hear him groaning to his feet, shuffling his aluminum walker across the floor, and then— when he opened the door to nothing but a clear Carolina sky— cursing with an animation and vigor that belied his presumed fragility. Why, he wanted to know, couldn't children leave an old man alone to die in peace?

Then one day, the story goes, the old man set a trap for his tormentors. All day he waited with his shotgun near the door and when he heard childish giggles and the squeak of sneakers on his porch, he jerked the trigger and blasted a big hole through the world before the boys could even press the doorbell.

A young woman screamed—the warm blood of her children, the old man's grandchildren, greased the porch. They had come that very day to surprise their grandfather; one version held that his daughter had decided to invite the old man to come back and live with her family in their big house in the country.

As pat and predictably horrible as that story seems now, at the time, it held a real and terrible power over us. It instructed us that playful cruelty could have serious consequences, that there were adults in the world who weren't like our mothers and fathers, people who might not use good judgment. It suggested that we lived in a world where the slaughter of innocents was a possibility.

And though we laughed about it, there was some nervousness attached. We thought a lot about that bitter, sad old man on the other side of the door, waiting to redress some injury.

In those days we were free, on Halloween, to slip away from our homes and range all over town in gangs, to cross the railroad tracks and plunge down streets where no one we knew lived. We were good kids, for the most part, brought up to say "sir" and "ma'am" even when we were dressed as little monsters. There were no real tricks in our repertoire, but then no one ever refused us our booty; we always returned with grocery bags heavy with Black Cow and Zero bars, with popcorn balls and wads of taffy twisted in orange wax paper.

Still there were steps we would not walk up, houses that were too dark or too odd to chance. We stayed out of the trailer park, not for any reason we could understand but because our parents told us to, and we left the big house with the iron fence and the big dogs alone, even though—or perhaps because—it was decorated for the season, with a realistic skeleton and an unconvincing ghost that looked like a basketball shrouded with a bedsheet and hung from a tree.

After dark, we went only to the places where porch lights burned. By 9 P.M. we'd be home, to dump our bags out on the table and to negotiate trades, to try to pawn off our hard candy on our siblings by telling them we sincerely believed the centers were soft. Then our mothers would take most of the candy and put it in a big, communal bowl anyway, and put it on the top of the refrigerator so that when no one was around we would have to climb onto the countertop to reach it.

Then we would pad off to our rooms in flannel nightclothes, with a secret cache of Slo-pokes and Sugar Babies in finger-reach beneath our beds. And through our open windows autumn-bitten air would blow, waving our cowboy curtains, and moonlight would make soft shadows on the wall. We'd slowly soak ourselves down into a delicious gray pool of drowse, exhausted, excited, and perhaps a little stomach-sick. We were such proud and fearless children.

It cannot, of course, be that way anymore. It can't be, largely because we have grown up to imagine monsters everywhere, to despair of a world gone wrong.

It hardly matters that what killed the Halloween we used to know was a rumor, a story like the one that worried us as children. They said people were handing out deadly treats, adulterating Pixie Stix powder with rat poison and pushing razor blades into apples. It doesn't matter that it never happened, that there has never been a documented case of a child being injured by a doctored apple, that there was only a single case of Pixie Stix poisoning and that was by a deranged father who wanted to murder his son to collect on an insurance policy.

It doesn't matter that all those stories about Satanists kidnapping babies and murdering children and running their own day-care centers turned out to be fabrications.

It doesn't matter that those things don't happen because we are able to imagine that those things could happen. Because it is a simple enough precaution to X-ray an apple—these days would anyone even give a neighbor's child a treat that didn't come sealed in some tamper-resistant packaging? We know there is evil in the world, bad people with the capacity to do harm to those we love. We hear the sirens at night; some of us hear the crackle of gunfire.

We wouldn't let our children walk around the block alone in daylight, let alone let them scramble over blocks where strangers live. Children must be escorted these days; they must be protected.

This is all understandable, all very reasonable. Children are not something one takes chances with; they needn't take part in this pagan ritual. They can go to parties at Chuck E. Cheese; they can watch scary movies on the VCR; they can pretend it's Halloween and go to sleep behind iron burglar bars. Everything will be all right.

When the old mapmakers came to the margins of the known world, they sometimes wrote a legend on the blank territories: "Where Monsters Be." These days we imagine that behind every door lies an uncharted and unknowable country, potentially a tangle of hurt and rage, seething in the darkness and waiting for an object on which to vent its lethal pique. That is the scariest story I know.

(1994)

125 •

Hating the Dodgers

My father was a Dodger fan. My earliest memory involves a blue and white T-shirt emblazoned with the team's logo. In those days, of course, they were the Brooklyn Dodgers, though they wouldn't be for long.

He knew well those postwar teams, those names that ganged together in a kind of incantation: Furillo, Reese, Snider, Hodges, later Robinson and Campenella and Newcombe and Drysdale and the others. The Dodgers were my father's team, the team of his adolescence and young adulthood, and though it was a long way from Asheville, North Carolina, to Ebbets Field, he mourned their move to the coast.

Though he thought O'Malleys' desertion was a cynical and soulless thing to do, he soon forgave the Dodgers, and later, when we also moved west he would take me to games at Dodger Stadium in Chavez Ravine. We always arrived early enough to watch batting and infield practice, and he took advantage of the time to instruct me on the small points that made a man a ballplayer. For a time he had been a professional shortstop, small but with quick wrists that gave him surprising power. He had favorites, and the players he particularly admired reflected his own ethic of duty and work.

He liked Wally Moon because the big man had adjusted his left-handed stroke to take advantage of the short left-field wall in the Los Angeles Coliseum, where the Dodgers played their first year out of Brooklyn. He liked Maury Wills because he saw in the scrappy shortstop a man of meager natural gifts who had made himself first into a switch-hitter and then into an All-Star. Junior Gilliam similarly impressed him—especially when, in 1965, at the age of thirty-six, he came out of retirement to hit .280 and (temporarily) solve the Dodgers' perennial third-base problem.

The year 1965 was also the year that Tommy Davis broke his right ankle early in the season, depriving the Dodgers of their starting left-fielder and one of the game's best hitters. To replace him, manager Walter Alston called up a thirty-one-year-old veteran named Lou Johnson. Johnson had spent thirteen unspectacular seasons in the minor leagues, but that year he went on to hit a dozen home runs and drive in fifty-eight runs—not an inconsequential amount for a team that scored as infrequently as the Dodgers. My father became a Lou Johnson fan in 1965.

That was the year, ironically perhaps, when I learned to hate the Dodgers.

I would like to be able to write that I hated them because they broke my father's heart, but that would be romantically inaccurate. I was never a Dodger fan, probably because the Dodger teams I first became aware of were squads built on speed and pitching, finesse teams that manufactured runs and won and lost "boring" games by one-run margins.

I liked the Boston Red Sox, the Cincinnati Reds of Frank Robinson and Vada Pinson, and—of all teams—the vainglorious New York Yankees with Mantle and Maris and Yogi Berra and Tom Tresh. Later I would come to love the Pittsburgh Pirates with the sullen, masterful Roberto Clemente.

But most of all, I liked the San Francisco Giants. I liked them because, most of the time, they were the team that was playing the Dodgers when we went to Dodger Stadium. I liked them because my uncle lived in San Francisco—he took me to games at Candlestick.

I loved Willie Mays and Orlando Cepada and Willie McCovey and, beyond all comprehension, a little outfielder named Mateo Alou, who—in 1965—definitely seemed the least of three brothers. (Once, I think in 1966, the Alou brothers, Felipe and Jesus and Matty, comprised the Giant's outfield for an inning—the only time in major league history brothers have accomplished that.) The Giants were, as the team name implies, big and thundery. They were hitters mainly, though they had the elegant Juan Marichal, and they were not so subtle as the Dodgers. I mean those fierce old Giants no disrespect when I say they were a boy's team; the Dodgers were for more sophisticated tastes.

Yet, if I am honest, I must admit I loved the Giants out of mischief, too. I know it annoyed my father that I preferred Marichal to Koufax, a Mays double to a Wills bunt-and-steal. I took some delight in rooting for the Dodgers' mortal enemies—it made those games more interesting.

What everyone remembers about 1965 is the ugliness that occurred on August 22 at Candlestick Park. Giant pitcher Marichal went after Dodger catcher John Roseboro with a bat, cutting his head and touching off a fourteen-minute riot. Marichal was suspended for eight games and forbidden from accompanying the Giants on their final trip to Los Angeles on September 6 and 7. I remember my father's anger that any man would use a bat on another player, particularly one so gentlemanly as the quiet Roseboro.

I remember a flush of shame, but it passed. That year Mays hit fifty-two home runs, and McCovey thirty-nine, and though the pennant race was close—there were no play-offs then—the Giants reeled off a fourteen-game winning streak in September and moved ahead of the Dodgers by four-and-a-half games.

But then the Dodgers finished the season by winning fifteen of their last sixteen, overtaking my Giants and winning the pennant by two games.

My father, I remember, was exceedingly kind at the end. Yet something went bitter in my young heart—the disappointment stung so badly I cried.

It is spring again, and I am no longer the youngest person in the office. Probably most of the folks around here were yet to be born in 1965, even those who care about a thing as picayune as baseball probably wonder at my affinity for a team that can only be reassembled in my imagination. Where have you gone, Tito Fuentes? Or you, Jim Ray Hart?

The game is different, these days, not better, not worse, but different. Curt Flood freed the slaves, then went off to Spain to wear a beret and paint in the cafes. He is one of my heroes, too, but he changed this game.

Now we root for players more than teams, if we root at all. I still love the snap of baseballs through bright air, the rub of leather, the pregnancy of a curve ball about to break . . .

But I no longer hate the Dodgers. And somehow, there is something sad in that.

(1994)

Spook Story

Nights are blacker in east Texas. Headlights grope along an oatmeal-colored road threading through a murky piney forest. A road from nowhere to nowhere, through eventless counties wet and dry, with heat lightning blinking in the thunderless north sky.

It is cheap to live out here, off this road and down a gravel track. More house for the money, and your only neighbors are like-minded folk. They lift a finger in greeting when they drive past, they don't drop in uninvited, but they call if they see a strange car parked in front of your house. They call, a yellow porch light—yellow to shoo off bugs—ignites, and you step through the screen door to see who's come to call. You buy your groceries in a town called Uncertain; you've been to college, you know about irony and stuff.

• • •

Some stories are like cancer. You carry them around and they eat at you. You try to kill them, you take your medicine, you do what's necessary. And when what's necessary doesn't work, you take extraordinary measures.

No one believes your story. They say they believe you believe it, but they don't, not really. They couldn't. It's not their fault—sometimes even you think you've made it up.

But it happened. It was long ago and you were six. Your brother was with you, though he won't talk about it now. He became a preacher, your brother; he's said the whole thing was made up by your mother, to get attention, because she was mentally unstable, that it never happened, that you and he told the story because she made you tell it.

But you know that's not true. You know your brother knows; the last time you talked with him face to face, years ago, his eyes gave him away. He was scared as you, looking for his own hole to crawl into, looking to get away from you, his own flesh and blood, because you were together when it happened, because he can't understand how you both had the exact same dream.

•   •   •

It was when you were living up north. In the 1950s, when the skies were full of strange objects, when things like this were getting into the newspapers. When people were more credulous, when rocketry had about it a kind of pure blue burn.

Like in that movie, you and your brother—your eight-year-old brother—awoke and without a word to one another walked out into the yard in the middle of the night. It was a cool still night, and you remember the softness of pajama flannel, the cool smoothness of the pebble you scrunched your toes around. You remember the light, hanging in the air, the Coleman lantern of the gods, a soft glow, not blinding, something you could look at, something comforting, something somehow not even very surprising.

You both walked toward it and followed it a hundred yards or so, until it dipped over a hill. You climbed the hill and scooted down on your butt, you and your brother. You both saw them. There's no way he can claim he never saw them. He saw them, same as you.

It is ridiculous to describe them. Ridiculous. They had the big heads, the big eyes—let's just say whoever did that movie, that *Close Encounters* movie, they did their research. That's what they looked like. Three or four of them. And the light, fuzzy and oblong, a few feet off the ground.

They didn't scare you. You—you and your brother—moved toward them. One saw you. He lifted something like a finger, not, come to think of it, unlike the way your neighbors now lift their fingers when they pass you on the road.

You thought he meant come closer. So you took another step . . .

•   •   •

It was just before dawn when you woke up. They were gone and you were sore. You felt sort of sunburned—from your face to your feet. You scrambled home, you and your brother; you went in through the back door and climbed back in bed and began to shake and cry.

Your brother woke up your mom. He told her what happened, he told her and she ran to your room, not understanding, not believing, just stunned. You felt hot to her touch. There were pine needles all over your back, all stuck to the bed. Your brother was OK. He had been a few feet behind you when what he was already calling the "shock wave" hit. He had been "knocked out unconscious," he told her, "knocked out unconscious."

The doctor said it was the damnedest thing. You were bruised from forehead to feet. Nothing serious, it was just like you had flattened yourself against a wall. And the nausea? That was probably just from overexcitement.

•   •   •

Telling the story was a mistake. It got in the newspaper; it got in many newspapers. Reporters from all over called; some even showed up at your mother's house. It got bad. The kids in school taunted you, giggled, made fun, said you made it all up to get on television. It got better, then it would start up again. Other kids weren't allowed to come to your house; the sheriff told your mom he was thinking about charging her with filing a false report. People said something was wrong with you, that maybe your brain wasn't wired properly, that you weren't quite right.

You never said they were spacemen. You said you didn't know who or what they were or what they wanted. You wanted a perfectly logical explanation; it wasn't your fault there wasn't one.

You had to move. You moved and your mom changed everybody's name. And you quit talking about it, even among yourselves. About the time your brother hit thirteen, he started saying the whole thing was a made-up story. He said your mom had had you both hypnotized or something, that she was trying to make money, to get on Ed Sullivan.

Later, he became a preacher. He told the story then, but he told it in a different way. He said it had all been a "con job," that when he was a little boy his mother had tried to make him into a freak. He built several sermons around his version of the story; he recorded them and sent you the tapes. It made your head swim.

You just tried to quit thinking about it. You went to school, got a job, got married. It was a few years before you told your wife the story. You were surprised how well she took it. She didn't believe you at first, but she knows you are a serious man. She believes you now. Or maybe she just believes that you believe it. Those things don't bother you much anymore. Everybody has their little quirks. If people want to think you're just a little bit nutty on this topic, well that's fine.

There are nights when you sit out back and look off into the big silver-peppered emptiness and you get the feeling that you're looking into your own soul, that there's something unknowable and unapproachable out there, something humbling and worthy of your awe. Something as irrational and perfect as the truth.

(1994)

The Bulletproof
Myth of Bonnie
and Clyde

The death car came to Goldsboro, North Carolina, when I was ten years old and just big enough to be dropped off at the matinee on Saturday afternoons. It was parked inside a long trailer which some entrepreneur had pulled up on a sidewalk in front of the theater. It cost fifty cents to go inside and stick your finger into rusty bullet holes. Various small arms were mounted in glass cases, and laying across the back seat of the sand-colored Model A were two gold-painted "death masks."

I know about the death masks only because after I passed through the exhibit the man who was tearing tickets asked me if I had seen them. I told him I hadn't, and he let me go back in for free. I looked at them hard, and they have lodged in my memory. They were bland, mundane and featureless—one vaguely female—and it wasn't very long after I saw them that I decided they must have been fakes. Maybe the car was a fake, too, but the bullet holes were real and horrible.

And Bonnie Parker and Clyde Barrow were also real and horrible; and they drove a car very much like the death car into the inevitable fusillade of bullets along this gray tweed highway eight miles south of Gibsland, Louisiana, one May morning in 1934. Bonnie died with a movie tabloid at her feet, a bacon-and-tomato sandwich in her mouth, and a Browning automatic rifle across her lap; Clyde was driving without his shoes.

On this cold day under gunmetal skies, the tombstonelike historical marker—pocked by time and vandals since its erection in 1968 by the Bienville Parish Police Jury—seems particularly sorry and banal:

At this site, May 23, 1934, Clyde Barrow and Bonnie Parker were killed by law enforcement officials.

•   •   •

Though this is not a particularly awe-inspiring spot, it happened here, where a dim road tops a gentle hill and then breaks for the horizon like a convict for the far high wall; some of these pine trees witnessed the ambush, heard the death gurgles, watched the cautious deputy—nervous even after hundreds of rounds had sliced through the Ford—tiptoe down the ditch bank, lean in the window, and cut the ignition.

They found six inches of garbage in the floorboard of the car—sandwich wrappers, napkins, newspapers, and other road debris, the byproducts of a lifestyle based on fear and mobility. An inventory of the car turned up $507 in cash, a second Browning rifle, three government-issue submachine guns, six Browning automatic pistols, a .38 caliber revolver, two sawed-off automatic shotguns, two thousand rounds of ammunition, fifteen automobile license plates, and a saxophone.

Most of the weapons and ammunition came from a daring daylight raid on the National Guard Armory at Forth Worth. The saxophone was Clyde's—he presumably liked to play whenever the outlaws could catch their breath between filling-station holdups.

This was what the fugitive couple had to show for two years driving the backroads of the southern Midwest, killing and robbing and taunting their thick-limbed pursuers in the press. Bonnie posed for photographs, hitching her leg up on a bumper and waving a handgun, or smoking cigars with a shotgun tucked under her arm. She mailed off her mawkish poetry to be printed in the papers while Clyde wrote a sincere-sounding letter to Henry Ford praising the V-8 Model A's virtues as a getaway vehicle. They were more than outlaws, they were an efficient public-relations engine.

• • •

And theirs was a ruthless, wicked run that became the stuff of legend, echoed by Kerouac and in hundreds of B movies, and in a few better films, Fritz Lang's *You Only Live Once,* and, of course, Arthur Penn's 1968 blockbuster *Bonnie and Clyde,* the Warren Beatty–Faye Dunaway vehicle whose opening surely must have coincided with the appearance of the death car in Goldsboro.

It hardly matters that these murderers were not attractive people.

Clyde was a scrawny, screwed-up seventeen-year-old car thief who was sold to a cellmate for a carton of cigarettes during his first stint inside the penitentiary. Bonnie married safecracker Roy Thorton at sixteen and tattooed his name and a pair of hearts on her right thigh before he went away to prison—for ninety-nine years, for good. She then worked in cafes and police bars in Kansas City and Dallas before taking up with the man who was later to become Clyde Barrow's lieutenant, Ray Hamilton. There is some speculation that Hamilton was Clyde's real love interest, that perhaps the only gang members who never shared a bed from time to time were Bonnie and Clyde.

•   •   •

But the facts are mildly superfluous; in the legend-building matrix, images are supreme. Clyde's weak features and Bonnie's birdish looks blur across the twin filters of time and grainy photographs. Warren Beatty rolling across the gravel, a muzzle flashing in his hand, is more real to us than Clyde slumped behind the wheel, dead before he realized he was ambushed. Bonnie and Clyde drove dead into the fabric of American road myth; they are forever young, forever beautiful, and forever dangerous in our collective consciousness.

After the barrels cooled, they hauled the bodies and the death car to Arcadia, stopping at a school to let the children peer into the car and rub their small hands across it, the ruptured sheetmetal an object lesson in what fate befalls the evildoer. They laid Bonnie and Clyde out in front of Conger's furniture store, and thousands of people came from two and three states away to review the riddled corpses. They found the owner of the bullet-violated Ford—within a few weeks she came down from Kansas City and took her car away.

Maybe it was the same car I encountered that afternoon in Goldsboro, though I have been told there were dozens of death cars making the rounds of county fairs and carnivals around the country. It is difficult to see what difference it makes; it was a reasonable facsimile, a good story to tell.

And when something has passed into mythology, it is invulnerable to truth.

(1986)

135 •

New Orleans

A week after Mardi Gras you can still find strings of plastic beads in the gutter along St. Charles Avenue or drooping in candy colors from tree limbs. Becalmed, the city yet feels stormful, as though the ions were choosing sides and gathering.

There is no place so murderously lovely as New Orleans. We sit on the second-story porch of a hotel called the Columns with a bottle of Winn-Dixie wine and watch the Boschian parade pass. Streetcars clack, and students from Loyola and Tulane pad by in running outfits. Tourists wander up, checking their guidebooks to see if this is, in fact, the place where Louis Malle filmed *Pretty Baby*. (Indeed it is, sir; the ghost of twelve-year-old Brooke Shields still haunts the mahogany stairwell. Sometimes at night you can hear her squirming into her Calvins beneath the stained-glass dome.)

This hotel was built in 1883, and from the street it looks as though it might be made of stone. It is *tromp l'oeil*—white enamel gleams hard off the wood.

While they say it is the only surviving example of Italianate architecture in the Garden District, there are grand houses all up and down St. Charles and its neighboring streets. Some of these houses have rooms twenty-two feet square. They were all built long ago, by people long dead. They will not endure, either; eventually they will slip into disrepair and be boarded up, and later pulled down, by man or by the elements.

Looking at these mansions, one might be reminded of those medieval cathedrals that took lifetimes to build. A mason would start to work on a project with no hope of ever seeing its completion, sustained by faith in an appreciative God.

Some of these houses have stood for nearly as long as it took to build one of those muscular cathedrals, though it is hard to see how they can last another century. These days it must be all but impossible to find someone to polish all that brass and dust that scroll work. Their paint peels, and heavy, gray air-conditioning units jut from the second-story windows of some of them, postmodern gargoyles meant to ward off the demon heat.

New Orleans is a city with noble rot. She could do with a lick of paint, but she is comfortable with her maturity. As rotten, corrupt, and wicked as she seems at times, New Orleans has no problems with self-esteem. She knows how time rounds all corners and works soft abrasive fabrics. New Orleans flows across your skin like a favorite frayed shirt, with sorrow in the weave.

Sorrow is always about in New Orleans; it hangs in the humidity. In just a few more weeks the city will go hot and the brandied air will stick in your throat like a mumbled apology. In just a few weeks, the tourists will be in their shorts and tank tops, and the thinned-out trees will blast green. Now is the time to be in New Orleans, during Lent, when hangovers are nursed with chicory coffee and sins are repented.

Our friend is out of town. He is a big-shot writer, and he has commitments, some kind of conference in Boulder, Colorado. He left regrets on our answering machine. It is OK. I have been here often enough, I know my way around. I know what streets we shouldn't walk down (though we invariably walk down them anyway). Karen knows a good bar in the Quarter where the drinks are nearly free. We have a list of new restaurants we want to try, a few old ones we want to go back to, twenty-two late-period Monets hanging in the Museum of Art, and even a couple of movies unlikely to play in the movie houses back home in Little Rock.

But for now it is enough to sit on the porch, cheap Gamay Beaujolais swishing tannic through our teeth. The car is in a safe place. We have no appointments to keep. And although the hot water barely dribbles out of the shower head, if you add a touch of cold the pressure is good enough.

Nothing really comes too easy in the Big Easy; you still have to work—or pay—for your comfort. The front page of the *Times-Picayune* is screaming about crime. Crime is bad, and there are desperate people everywhere. Perhaps, the newspaper suggests, the young mayor with the familiar name should reconsider a policy that requires police officers to live within the city's limits or forfeit any chance of promotion.

Crime is a problem here; people are being killed every day. It is all due to drugs, to the illicit churning of an alternate economy. Even on Canal Street you meet hard characters these days, men in pawn-shop jewelry and peaked hoods. The chamber of commerce is worried that it might affect the tourist trade. And, for what it's worth, the son of the Orleans Parish district attorney is a pop star. I still think of Harry Connick as a politician, not a Sinatra sound-alike.

It is a three-mile walk to the French Quarter. We do it a couple of times a day. The weather is mild and breezy, and there is no other way to really know a city but through its sidewalks. That's the reason Los Angeles always feels so alien—there is no place to walk, no pedestrian center, no center of civic gravity. You get to know a city through the soles of your feet. You walk it.

We walk it even when it's awkward to walk it, when we're skittering like beetles across the torn-up streets under the overpass or the wide lanes of Claiborne Avenue. We walk past huddled homeless and street preachers and Watchtower hawkers, through the fetid warehouse blocks between the Garden District and the Central Business District, past empty grandstands that just a week before were jammed with people crowded in to watch the parades.

Of course, if you wait long enough another parade will always come along. And down on Magazine Street the Irish are gearing up their St. Patrick's Day celebration. Roughnecks from Algiers ride in double-tiered floats, tossing beads and trinkets and heads of cabbage to the crowd.

It is not so easy to catch a vigorously hurled cabbage; you generally need two hands. Between us we catch six of them, along with a potato, an apple, and a banana Moon Pie. We place the vegetables (we keep the Moon Pie) in the shopping bags of old folks who wait beatifically in lawn chairs; their smiling, patient faces warmed by a mild sun.

One supposes the Lord is pleased with New Orleans.

(1994)

Approximately Huddie Ledbetter

The Blues, like the past, is alien ground where we cannot walk, though we can pretend to know something about it. Drive far enough into the dark in any direction and you might come to a still-standing husk of a colored juke. If you are brave and decent enough, you might pull into that crunchy gravel lot, kill your lights—ghosts and angels shine silver in the high beams— and hunch your shoulders against the cold. You might, after a moment of hesitation, stamp inside.

There will be a roar of oily warmth, then a hot sickness rising in your brow. You will notice the stove, proud and thick with blackness, and some frisky whiteheaded domino players shimmering mirage-like through a curtain of heat. You drip on the dry, splintery floor, creak over and shuck your heavy coat onto a formica-topped table. You cradle a cue and drink some aluminum-tainted beer and marvel at the little pills of sweat even as the wind infiltrates the tarpaper-covered walls.

These old men, their eyes run yellow and kindly, may be deferential to you, but there is something like hate in the hard eyes of the younger men in their poor clothes and thin jackets. Maybe there are reasons you don't go to places like this, and maybe this is a mistake. Maybe you have committed some unpardonable offense.

Now something sad catches like a fishhook in your throat, maybe it is grief. Maybe you think about a lover you will never see again, maybe you think about the unbearable horror you try never to think about. Maybe you are lonesome now.

That, White Boy, is the approximate truth of the Blues.

•   •   •

As the three men made their way across the river bottoms near New Boston, Texas, the Great War in Europe was winding down. It was not their war; they were musicians on their way to a dance. They were nominally partners, and it is among such men that things like what happened usually happen.

Alex Griffin said something about a woman—a prostitute—with whom Will Stafford had taken up. Stafford was offended, and the guitar player, a powerful heavy man with a smile-shaped scar ringing his neck, stepped in.

Maybe Stafford's last mistake was fingering his pistol, and maybe that is only the story they tell. All the court records say is that Walter Boyd shot Will Stafford through the head—killing him. On December 13, 1917, Boyd was charged with murder and assault with intent to kill. Six months later he was on his way to the Shaw State Prison Farm, a thirty-three-year-old man facing a thirty-year sentence. What we know that the court did not was that Walter Boyd had already escaped a Harrison County chain gang—that his name wasn't Walter Boyd. It was Huddie Ledbetter.

Born and reared on Caddo Lake near the Texas-Louisiana border, Ledbetter was the son of a decent man, a church secretary who managed to purchase sixty-eight acres of lakeside land between Longwood and Mooringsport, Louisiana. Young Huddie was caught between the sweet redemption promised by the church and the lowdown swagger of the songster's life. Early on he demonstrated a facility for music, learning the rudiments of the keyboard by the time he was eight years old by playing a single-key accordion called a "windjammer." Later he played some piano and organ.

He learned guitar from men like Jim Fagin and Bud Coleman, and by the time he was in his teens he was carrying a Colt revolver and a battered old guitar to rural house dances and breakdowns. By sixteen, he was an occasional performer in the brothels and on the streets of Shreveport's St. Paul's Bottoms. He was also, by most accounts, a surly and arrogant man—the apocryphal story is that he came to be called "Leadbelly" after being gut shot by a Caddo Parish deputy sheriff's shotgun.

Badman legends are plentiful and ultimately superfluous, in light of Ledbetter's subsequent place in American music. More important things happened on Fannin Street than the whoring and boozing; it was there that Ledbetter was exposed to the rolling barrelhouse styles of piano men who used heavy, walking bass figures. Ledbetter was to transpose these styles to the guitar—in the process he created a new vernacular for the instrument.

Ledbetter learned to tune his twelve-string instrument low, with the three highest-sounding pairs of strings tuned in unison, the fourth and fifth pairs tuned an octave apart and the sixth pair two octaves apart. This enriched the range of his instrument and allowed him to imitate the rumbling, full sound of the barrelhouse pianists he had heard. For the most part, he was a rhythm player, but he wove quick arpeggios and riff into his patterns so seamlessly his recordings often sound as though two guitars (or more) are playing. Today, even those who know his secrets cannot always fathom the depth of his playing.

Still, the most important thing Ledbetter learned on Fannin Street was how to give voice to that inexpressible hurt some people call the Blues. His teacher was a fat, bland-looking blind man from about eighty miles south of Dallas. A man ten years his junior, a man with an eerie, neck-prickling talent.

His name was Lemon Jefferson.

●　　●　　●

It may be nothing more than a chauvinism of the sighted, but it has often been implied that the blind are somehow "gifted" with an especially sensitive nature, that perhaps they are capable of hearing things outside the range of ordinary people.

Blind musicians—especially if they are black men—are often viewed, rather romantically and patronizingly, as *savants*, but the overriding, overlooked reasons blind instrumentalists have played such a large part in shaping popular music are economic reasons. Music is an occupational avenue the blind can pursue on almost equal footing. A blind boy was unable to work in the fields, and a poor blind boy was unable to lay up and be taken care of by his family.

When Jefferson met Huddie Ledbetter, the blind man was just another struggling street musician, too independent to allow himself to be led around, too cussed to be partners with anyone for very long. Even so, the big men played together in Dallas, Shreveport, in dozens of anonymous tonks and train stations, and the faceless crowds who sat and drank or danced and sweated through the sets the men played may have guessed they were witnessing something rare. Jefferson's hands scampered over the fretboard, echoing the high keen of his voice, in what must have been a marked contrast with Ledbetter's (then) warm tenor and accomplished playing.

Still, Ledbetter was just a songster, a player of reels and sentimental ballads. Jefferson scraped him hard against the Blues, and the collision left an indelible stain.

• • •

They say that in 1925, while incarcerated at Shaw State Prison Farm, Huddie Ledbetter gave a command performance for Texas governor Pat Neff. A few months later, whether through coincidence or because he sang so well what the governor wanted to hear, he was a free man. He moved back near his family home in Louisiana.

"Huddie was always real popular in Mooringsport," Florida Combs, the singer's second cousin, said. "And he was the only one ever to play his way out of prison." Combs's sister, Pinkie Williams, insists that after Ledbetter was released from Shaw he joined the Shiloh Baptist Church—a claim which is partially confirmed by an aside on the Library of Congress recordings when Ledbetter tells John Lomax he joined the church "for about a week" after his release.

While Ledbetter still played parties and dances (often with Combs's and Williams's father, Edmond "Son" Ledbetter), there was a darker edge to his music. The post-prison Huddie Ledbetter was more likely to perform his own material, edgy songs soaked with sin and madness. "Never has a white man had the Blues," he once said, "'cause nothing to worry about."

If Lemon Jefferson gave him a voice for the Blues, then the prison farm gave him the proper heart.

Then he was arrested again. This time it was for assault with intent to commit murder. On February 28, 1930, Huddie Ledbetter was sentenced to a second prison term.

• • •

Folk archivists John and Alan Lomax—then transversing the country making field recordings of folk singers for the Library of Congress—found Ledbetter in the Louisiana State Penitentiary at Angola in 1933.

"We were amazed by his mastery of his great, green-painted twelve-string guitar," Alan Lomax later wrote. "We were deeply moved by the flawless tenor voice which rang out across the cotton field like a big sweet-toned trumpet. We believed 'Leadbelly' when he said, 'I'ze the king of all the twelve-string guitar players in the world.'"

After recording dozens of original field hollers and work songs, Ledbetter reputedly asked the Lomaxes to take an acetate copy of one of his songs to Louisiana governor O. K. Allen. The song—later copyrighted as "Governor O. K. Allen"—asked, in no uncertain terms, for a commutation. Though the Lomaxes indicated they did give the governor a copy of the song, there is no strong evidence to indicate he ever heard it. Even so, Ledbetter (along with hundreds of other prisoners from Louisiana's overcrowded system) was released in 1934.

John Lomax later told the *New York Herald Tribune* about meeting Ledbetter after his release:

> On August 1, Leadbelly got his pardon. On September 1, I was sitting in a hotel in Texas when I felt a tap on my shoulder. I looked up and there was Leadbelly with his guitar, his knife and a sugar sack packed with all his earthly belongings. He said, "Boss, I came here to be your man. I belong to you."
>
> I said, "Well, after all, I don't know you. You're a murderer. . . . If some day you decide on some lonely road that you want my money and my car, don't use your knife on me. Just tell me and I'll give them to you. I have a wife and a child back home and they'd miss me."

Lomax's version of events is suspect and undoubtably as self-serving as it is colorful. This color was no doubt injected to help establish the burlesque act which Ledbetter's career was to become during the next few years. Like King Kong plucked from Monster Island, Huddie Ledbetter became "Leadbelly"—a nickname his descendants dislike and say he never cared much for, either—and was displayed as a curiosity to the genteel citizens of New York.

A tour of northern colleges—beginning with Bryn Mawr—was arranged, and over the next few years, the "Sweet Singer of the Swamplands" toured the country under the tutelage of the Lomaxes, recording a little, baring his teeth, and winking to his masters.

Ledbetter's criminal background was as much a draw as his playing and singing. His dangerous edge was always emphasized —John Lomax called him a "natural" with "no idea of money, law or ethics . . . possessed of virtually no self-restraint."

This relationship between the Lomaxes and Ledbetter was, however, symbiotic. Though Ledbetter was undoubtably exploited (for a while he served as John Lomax's valet, and Alan Lomax shared most of Ledbetter's copyrights and later wrote an offensive and inaccurate biography of the singer), the fiercely independent Ledbetter could not have gained a fraction of the popularity he eventually achieved without their help.

Through John Lomax's promotion, Ledbetter's 1935 wedding was featured in the newsreels, and eventually the ex-convict achieved a bit of celebrity in New York, becoming a minor don of Greenwich Village as he drifted into a circle of white performers including Woody Guthrie, Pete Seeger, and Cisco Houston.

For a time in the thirties, Ledbetter hosted his own radio show and was a frequent guest on Guthrie's show. He enjoyed a comfortable, grandfatherly lifestyle; then-struggling young bluesmen Brownie McGhee and Sonny Terry were just two of those sheltered and mentored by an expansive Huddie Ledbetter.

Yet the legend was to be punctuated by violence once again. In 1939, he was again arrested—for assault with murderous intent. Two years on Riker's Island ruined his voice and broke his spirit. After his release, he split time between New York and Hollywood, recording dozens of inferior sides.

Only Ledbetter's last recordings (*Leadbelly's Last Sessions, Vol. I* and *II*, Folkways) hint at the power of the 1933 field recordings—and they are most notable for the care and foresight folk music archivist Fredric Ramsey brought to the project. Recording in his New York apartment in 1948, Ramsey talked Ledbetter through the songs, soliciting the singer's comments and snatches of alternate approaches to the material. Ramsey intended to do more recording with Ledbetter, but the singer left for a brief tour of France in 1949.

Almost immediately upon his return, he was admitted to Bellevue Hospital, where he died on December 6, 1949.

• • •

Within months after Ledbetter's death, a white folk group, The Weavers, took a bowdlerized version of Ledbetter's "Goodnight Irene" to the number-one spot on the pop charts.

It was as close as Huddie Ledbetter ever came to a hit record.

•　　•　　•

For whatever it means, the poor quarter in Shreveport Huddie Ledbetter once haunted is now called Ledbetter Heights. It is a sad and disappointing sector, blighted and—except for a few laboratory houses, painted bright yellow and blue—colorless. A saint feeds the poor and shelters the homeless down there, but people still die violently, and women still rent their bodies down there, but the city bustles around the horror with unblinking eyes.

Ledbetter Heights hasn't changed much in seventy or so years; a lot of the old buildings still stand, blistered by time and neglect. If you dare to walk down there, you may feel strange and out of place. The music that gets played down there is usually made somewhere else, the blare of radios and cassette tapes. If you listen for it, you might detect Huddie's echoes.

Through technological contrivance, we can see the faces and hear the voices of the dead, but we cannot know the Past. On record, Huddie Ledbetter sometimes sounds like a drowning man; to modern ears accustomed to airbrushed tones his recording can seem to croak and rumble. There is a nervous, piercing quality to his voice when it climbs, and maybe the limits of the equipment of the day cloak the depth of his guitar playing.

You can clear a room by putting on one of his records; a lot of people don't understand.

But some do.

Huddie Ledbetter is dead, and he is buried near Mooringsport, in the land where he grew up. For the most part he is undisturbed, though occasionally pilgrims find him and visit as he sleeps. Sometimes someone will bring a guitar and sit beside the grave; they might play something they learned off a scratchy record, a snatch of something called the Blues.

(1988)

The Untidy Grave
of Blind Lemon
Jefferson

It doesn't happen for a long while—some days roll on as vacant and bland as a cloudless Texas sky—but sooner or later there is always another respectful-looking white boy, younger looking than the last one, prospecting through the headstones, straining to see something in the ancient feeble scratches, looking for something that is just not there.

There an old man will let him look a while, long enough to satisfy himself that this boy means to examine every tombstone in the yard, before he will speak.

"It not there," he will call across his newly turned garden. "It's acrost that fence yonder, in that stand of mesquite. It's way in the back and you got to look hard for it."

No, Blind Lemon Jefferson is not buried in the manicured, sweet-grassed Wortham Cemetery, nor does he rest in the sorry adjunct that abuts the old man's garden. He is buried in the old "Negro Cemetery," an acre or so of pastureland given over to the dead, stitched off by a rusted barb-wire fence. It is a discreet distance from the white folks' plot, and only the adventurous or the malicious would try to drive the last hundred yards or so, down a narrow track to the creosote wood and wire proscenium. It is not such a long walk from the highway, but the grass is snaky, knee-high, and rough as pumice on bare ankles.

The old man is right, one has to look hard to find it, a weed-ridden mound roughly as long and a third again as wide as a man. It is marked only by a historical marker dated 1967—a marker bent nearly double by vandals.

Maybe the marker was bent by the same vandals who took the headstone, though that doesn't seem quite right. More likely Blind Lemon Jefferson's monument leans against a paneled wall in the den of some blues appreciator—maybe he or she looks at it sometimes with a kick of regret and fear. Anyway, the bare-chested young man who was—until just a moment before—trying to whack down some overgrowth is now taking a break in the scant shade of an available mesquite. He draws long on an unfiltered cigarette and says he grew up in Wortham and can't remember the grave ever having a headstone.

Anyway, this is it. Blind Lemon is here, underneath this pad of sod—at least according to the historical commission. Maybe a little ambivalence is in order, here; Blind Lemon's was a sad and fuzzy life that ended either in 1929 or 1930, depending on the source.

We do know he was born near here, on a farm between the Trinity and the Navasota rivers, the last of seven children. We know he played parties and picnics—we know he was a blind beggar with a high, black, and desperate voice and hands that worked edgy runs down the treble strings of his guitar. We know his sound was as terrible as thunder and as delicate as morning mist, and if you've ever heard it you know how it feels to be lonesome and possessed by demons you can't quite name.

There are enough references to visual images in Lemon's work to suggest he was born sighted, but with eyes weak enough to spare him the cotton fields. He had to make a living with his gifts, and the pit that covered him also gave him time to practice and hone his craft.

Huddie "Leadbelly" Ledbetter used to tell people he hooked up with Blind Lemon in 1904, but that may have been a self-serving exaggeration designed to enhance Leadbelly's image. The men did travel together around 1915, with Leadbelly serving as valet as well as playing partner. One can only imagine the holy racket those twin guitars might have made on Shreveport's Fannin Street and in Dallas's Deep Ellum—in those days there were giants.

Blind Lemon broke out of that circuit first, and in Chicago he became one of the most prolific and commercially viable of the early bluesmen. He recorded as early as 1926, and at least seventy-nine of his compositions survive today, including the salacious "Black Snake Moan" and, ironically enough, "See That My Grave Is Kept Clean."

His records sold well throughout the South, and though his arpeggio guitar style was hardly original—a whole school of east Texas musicians mined a similar vein—dozens of later artists have acknowledged that their introduction to "hammering on" and "choking" notes came courtesy of Blind Lemon's recordings.

Despite his celebrity, Blind Lemon died of exposure on a Chicago street corner after he became disoriented (he refused to be led through the streets) and suffered a heart attack. Some accounts contend hundreds of people—bustling Christmas shoppers—stepped over or around him as he slowly froze to death.

But it is warm here. Warm and miserable. It took a while to find where Blind Lemon was buried—someone said there was a grave in Jefferson, Texas, someone else said they had visited his grave in Dallas.

They were wrong. It is here, just north of Wortham on Highway 14, segregated from the place where they plant the white people, in a raw and sorry grave.

But, the old man says, there always comes another to seek him out.

(1987)

Elvis Lives

Around 1981, Duke Presley brought his modest show to a whitewashed cinder-block American Legion hall near the almost imperceptible town of Elton—north of Jennings, west of Basile—in southwest Louisiana. Duke was there to help out the local volunteer fire department; he brought his threadbare jumpsuit, his tapes, and his sorry little PA system and stapled little photocopied posters on telephone poles all over Jefferson Davis Parish.

Duke's show was a tribute to his cousin—he said he was a cousin. He was, his posters claimed, "the only member of the Presley clan trying to carry on the family name: If you loved Elvis you will like Duke."

Most of that night is irretrievable, gone to time and whiskey. I might be missing some of the details; I can't recall whether it was summer or fall or winter, or whether I took a date to the show or whether or not we danced. I do remember that tickets cost three dollars but that I got in free because in those days I took photographs for the *Jennings Daily News* and sometimes for the *Lake Charles American Press,* too. Duke had set up his gear on a plywood riser about the size of a trailer-house bathroom, and there was a little square of dance floor in front of that. There were old varnished oak picnic tables scuffed and scratched and scorched by neglected cigarettes, and heavy men in tight periwinkle Ban-Lon and nervous women who clapped along and giggled whenever Duke would mop the sweat from his broad forehead with a polyester scarf and offer it to one of them. (After the show, he went 'round meekly and asked for them back.)

There was the skonky honk of feedback when Duke pointed the microphone toward the speaker, and I remember the way his bourbonny, approximate voice would occasionally catch a phrase just right—just the way Elvis did it—then gradually slide off, back into an indistinct, murmuring, touching, tentativeness.

I remember the hiss of the cassette tape Duke sang along with, the canned voices cushioning some of the choruses. I remember his nylon zippers, a shade whiter than the dingy polyester of his jumpsuit, and the way the flash gathered in his eyes in the photographs I took of him.

Those photographs were brutal; they threw heavy shadows on the wall inches behind Duke and washed out his dull animal face. They showed him up, his belly girth and his mascara. Duke didn't look like Elvis; he looked like a pathetic clown. He sloshed around his little stage like a water balloon—a sorry attempt made on the cheap in a homespun costume and plastic shoes and who kept getting his mike cord snagged on bench legs.

But in one photo, though, you could see something. Caught a little less than three-quarter face, his head lifted like a communant at the rail, Duke bore a faint but persistent resemblance to the King; maybe something in the line of his nose and angle of his jaw, maybe something as simple as the prayerfulness with which, for the sixteenth of a second it took to catch it, he held himself. You could look at Duke in that photo and see a germ of Elvisness.

●　　●　　●

I came to Oxford, Mississippi, to Ole Miss, to the First Annual International Conference on Elvis Presley (titled *In Search of Elvis, Music, Race, Religion, Art, Performance*) presented jointly by the school's Center for the Study of Southern Culture and Department of English, with about the same attitude I had approached Duke's tribute.

I expected pageantry and kitsch, a kind of communal groping for an impossible coherency and possibly even a moment or two of solemn beauty. I thought it might be fun, I was skeptical of its academic value, and someone else was paying.

But get real, man—Whither Elvis?

Elvis is out there, man, unavoidable, a trope, an icon, an American saint—there is Good Elvis, Bad Elvis, and, according to sinister biographer Albert Goldman, Little Elvis. Elvis Indivisible, the master of the unregenerate pose. Elvis to be loved and hated, mocked and venerated, sucked into the Bigface machine, pulverized, atomized, and pumped out into the ether-like perfume.

You don't need to look for Elvis, boy; Elvis finds you, yanks you out of a dream on a sticky summer night, hands you a sweaty bottle of cold co'cola, and drives you up to Memphis, Neal Cassidy speed-rapping all the way, his left hand easy on the pink Bakelite steering wheel, his right arm draped over the tuck-and-roll upholstery, his eyes concealed behind wraparound glasses while his heavy head points at you like a pistol so that you want to gently remind him to keep his eyes on the road but you don't.

You think about Elvis too much; he evaporates and you're left with nothing but a bunch of junky movies, stacks of digitally re-mastered CDs, a television special or two. Nothing but Graceland and ashtrays and Elvis soap on a rope. You're left with nothing but the commodities—you try to intellectualize this thing you fuck it up.

Maybe.

Maybe not.

> Rock music itself and talking about it with infinite seriousness are perfectly respectable. It has proved to be the ultimate leveler of intellectual snobbism.
>
> —Allan Bloom,
> *The Closing of the American Mind*

Vernon Chadwick is the Ole Miss professor of comparative literature who thought the conference up. Chadwick looks like a Doonesbury cartoon, the fighting-young-priest-who-can-talk-to-the-young. He wears black Guess jeans and T-shirts, his rusty hair academically long. He's got a beard and a good smile that gapes wider when he gets tense.

He's famous, sort of, for teaching a class that compared Herman Melville's trilogy of Polynesian novels with three Elvis films: *Blue Hawaii, Girls! Girls! Girls!*, and *Paradise, Hawaiian Style*—the kids called it "Melvis." Though Chadwick only taught that particular class once, most of the news stories that came out of the conference mentioned it, and most of them left the impression it was a continuing part of the Ole Miss English curriculum.

Chadwick admits he didn't try to disabuse the reporters of this notion; he knows it makes a good story. And he does use Elvis—his films and music—in his English classes to help his students "overcome the false distinction between high and popular culture."

"Elvis helps me understand the Middle Ages," he says, noting the way that some Elvis fans seize upon and venerate any tangible corporeal detritus left behind by their hero—artist Joni Mabe brought her prized Elvis wart and toenail to the conference—approximated the religious fervor of a medieval Catholic clutching the thighbone of a saint. "Elvis is very much like Jesus," Chadwick continues. "In a way, he transcended death—you have all these sightings of him which continue to this day."

People either believe in Elvis or they disbelieve in him. There are skeptics. And the idea of an academic conference on a figure like Elvis Presley is discomfiting to many. Since pop entered the academy in the mid sixties—coinciding with the rise of gender and ethnic studies—there have been those who doubted the probity of studying such cultural artifacts as sitcoms, detective novels, and Keanu Reeves.

In the mid to late eighties, the grumbling reached the level of *kulturkampf*, with the cultural conservatives' argument that college students were becoming increasingly disconnected with the Great Tradition of Western Civilization summarized succinctly in a book by the late University of Chicago philosophy professor Allan Bloom. Railing especially against the Dionysian noise of rock, *The Closing of the American Mind* became a runaway bestseller and furnished academic snobs with a ready-made argument against those who would elevate pop to art or study a phenomenon as low as the Hillbilly Cat.

"The academic left has debased the idea of culture by making Madonna into a subject as worthy of study as Shakespeare," says David Horowitz, a self-professed former campus radical turned conservative curmudgeon. "A lot of what passes for cultural studies is intellectual masturbation. Mickey Mouse is Mickey Mouse is what he is, but we don't need a Ph.D. thesis on it."

It probably didn't help that the six-day Elvis conference was scheduled to begin on August 6, just two days after Ole Miss's twenty-second annual symposium on the life and work of Oxford native son William Faulkner. Some—both at the university and in Oxford—thought the juxtaposition a little jarring; while Chadwick says that the organizers of the Faulkner conference were unfailingly supportive, he allows that he knows of several colleagues and Oxford residents who left town rather than encounter the expected Elvis influx.

"It's not the organizers," he says. "We both believe that the success of each conference would have helped the other. There were outsiders—bystanders—who identified with Faulkner and who've contributed to the class-based tension."

Bill Ferris, the director of the Center for the Study of Southern Culture, echoes Chadwick's remarks. "There is a deep and enduring division between the powerful elite, whose literary canon is represented by Faulkner, and the working class and blacks whose values are represented by Elvis," he says.

Oxford mayor John Leslie emerged as the point man for the anti-Elvis faction. When Ferris and Chadwick went before the city board to request that the city appropriate $7,000 to help fund the conference—2 percent of the conference's estimated $350,000 cost—the mayor argued against the city making any funds available to the conference. And when the board decided to give the center the money anyway, he vetoed the appropriation. Then they overrode his veto. He wasn't happy.

"It's just not becoming to the university," he says. "This city and Ole Miss have made a lot of progress in the last 25 years . . . I'm not anti-Presley (but) Elvis has no ties to Oxford. . . . In the early '50s he might have come through and ate at the Creme Cup. But that's all."

Leslie said he thought an Elvis conference would be more appropriate in Memphis, that he didn't want the University of Memphis trying to wrest Faulkner away from Ole Miss, and that the folks at the University of Memphis might not appreciate Ole Miss intruding on their academic turf.

Yet Chadwick—and much of Oxford—suspect a personal motive at the root of Mayor Leslie's opposition. His opponent in the last election was a society woman named Pat Lamar, a historic preservationist and in some eyes one of the chief architects of the cultural renaissance that has occurred in Oxford over the past twenty years or so—during which Oxford has been transformed from a sleepy little college town best known for the callout of federal troops in the wake of James Meredith's integration of Ole Miss in 1962, to a cultural hothouse and proving ground for writers as diverse as Donna Tartt, John Grisham, Barry Hannah, and Larry Brown.

Lamar, who hosted a dinner party for Elvis conference attendees, also happens to be Vernon Chadwick's sister.

"I think that's the story, that there's a personal motivation behind the mayor's opposition," Chadwick says. "There's no cultural choice between Faulkner and Elvis. . . . He's a typical mayor of the new South, concerned with economic growth at the expense of the indigenous culture—he's opposed cultural funding across the board and now he's hiding behind the Faulkner conference. He's never been a supporter of anything cultural going on in this city."

• • •

But what if they gave a conference and nobody came? When the conference was announced, Bill Ferris confidently predicted it would draw about 350 scholars. Mayor Leslie snorted that "they won't get half that—why would they come here when they can go to Memphis and see Graceland?"

In fact, the number of bodies that showed up was disappointing. There were almost as many members of the press in attendance during the first couple of days of the conference as registered attendees; about seventy academics and fans—mostly tenured faculty members—paid $350 for the privilege of attending the various lectures and performances.

Of course, the presence of the media ensured that the conference would draw attention. The Ole Miss public relations department estimated that about sixty reporters and technicians showed up during the conference, including all three major television networks, The Nashville Network, as well as representatives from dozens of newspapers including the *New York Times*, *Los Angeles Times*, *Chicago Tribune*, *Memphis Commercial Appeal*, and the *Baltimore Sun*.

Chadwick and Ferris, both preternaturally alert to the media possibilities, appeared on ABC's *Good Morning, America* to label the opening sessions a global "teleconference." In his opening remarks to the conference, kicking off the official academic phase of the conference, a somewhat subdued Chadwick expressed his hope that, by week's end, the Elvis conference would prove its credibility.

He needn't have worried so much. The previous day's concert, held at Ole Miss's Fulton Chapel, had won over most of the attendees, as well as a couple of hundred Presleyphiles-without-portfolio who just showed up at the door and paid their ten dollars. In retrospect, the opening concert provided a useful gloss for the entire conference. It started with gospel choirs and progressed through a middle period of Elvis impersonators—the worst of which was a damn sight more "professional" than Elvis's putative cousin Duke—and culminated in the realization of a kind of postmodern Elvis in the person of one Robert Lopez, an incandescent performer who bills himself as El Vez, "The Mexican Elvis."

So the concert surveyed both the authentic and the kitsch, the sacred and the profane, the stunted and the transcendental aspects of Elvis. Queen Elizabeth Weeden—whose mother worked with Gladys Presley at St. Joseph's Hospital in Memphis—and the Masonic Travelers out of Turrell, Arkansas, managed to work the half-full house to a frenetic pitch, muddying the waters with sensual, soul-wrenched versions of sacred songs.

Then they gave way to the impersonators, the Elvis manques in high hair and jumpsuits. Some people didn't like the impersonators.

Seiko Yagyu, who along with her husband, Nozumu, wrote the Japanese bestseller *Elvis: Symbol of Young America,* traveled from Tokyo to attend the conference. She found the impersonators tawdry and unnecessary.

"They don't impress me," she said. "There is only one Elvis."

Yet kitsch is an important part of the Elvis story, an essential ingredient to what the impersonators invariably call "his style of performance."

If you listen to the outtakes from young Elvis's sessions at Sun Studios, it's not difficult to discern a tendency for the callow singer to descend into facile schlock. Sam Phillips was, of course, the dominant presence in the studio, and he was—for as long as he held onto his contract—able to protect Elvis from himself. None of the sides Phillips released betray these frailties—to hear them you have to pick up the 1987 RCA re-packaging of the Sun tracks.

Elvis had no role models, no artists of "integrity"—no Dylans or Lennons—who preceded him and upon whom he could have modeled his career. He didn't aspire to Art—though he surely understood that pop music could move people the way literature and paintings could—he wanted to be a singer, an entertainer, a star. The successful singers of his day were crooners like Bing Crosby and Perry Como and especially Dean Martin, part-time movie stars absolutely outside what would become the rock 'n' roll ethos. Given the circumstances, it is hardly surprising the King of rock 'n' roll eventually abdicated his wild new realm for the safe and insular life of a sheik of Hollywood.

Chadwick wanted the Elvis impersonators there because he wanted to explore the entire Elvis continuum; he wanted Good Elvis as well as Bad, "kitsch" as well as "authentic."

Of course, it is probably impossible to separate authentic Elvis from kitsch Elvis. Anyone who has ever toured Graceland has probably entertained the notion that Elvis was authentically kitsch, that he came by his taste honestly. And the Elvis impersonators are, as a group, quite touching in their lack of professional cynicism. They seem to mean what they say when they (invariably) call their performances a tribute to the King.

"I know I could never be like Elvis and have Madison Square Garden up and cheering for me," Mark Hussman, who bills himself as the Apprentice Elvis, said. "It just makes me happy to entertain people in the same style as Elvis, to keep the music going for the kids who didn't get a chance to see him."

Hussman and his mentor, Rick Saucedo, traveled at their own expense from Chicago to attend the conference; they would go from Oxford to Memphis for the "Weep Week" ceremonies. ("What was I gonna do, sit home and drink beer?" a gruff Saucedo responded when asked why he had made the scene at Oxford.)

Elvis impersonators seem to seize on their hero's worst period—the Las Vegas-Aloha Elvis—and his worst material to present in their acts. Saucedo, acknowledged by his peers to be among the best of the Elvis impersonators, performs both "Girl Happy" and "Viva Las Vegas" in his set, complete with what seems an animatronic simulation of late Elvis dance moves. While he does sound right, not even Elvis could pull off an act so lame.

Maine dockworker Robert Washington, who bills himself as "The Black Elvis," specializes in a better time in Elvis's career; he replicates Elvis's performance on the 1968 comeback television special—he even incorporates some of Elvis's unfortunate tendencies into his act. When he blows the lyrics to "Jailhouse Rock" (how could anyone not know the lyrics to "Jailhouse Rock"?) he recovers with an Elvis-like shrug and wags his head in mock self-reproach. A chilling thought flits across the mind, what if the blown lyric is just part of the show?

Chadwick agrees that there are reasons the early Elvis, the Sun Sessions Elvis, would be difficult if not impossible to convincingly impersonate. First of all, the voice is higher, lighter than the 1970s version. Secondly, the performances are amazingly incandescent and frenetic—to jerk around so much would look ridiculous to audiences used to the more laid-back Elvis of later years.

But those are only technical problems; the real reason one sees so few performers attempting an early Elvis is because there is no way to reproduce that initial shock, the trans-racial energy, the moment of horror and dread and taboo-busting that the original Elvis occasioned. Modern audiences have trouble understanding just what it was about Elvis that caused White Citizens' Committees to form and condemn him—in so many ways it's difficult to imagine a world before Elvis.

"The Elvis of Choice is a much more comforting Elvis," Chadwick says. "While people voted for the Young Elvis for the postage stamp, I think that has to do with a different dynamic— the dream of eternal youth, the same dream that led a lot of the earlier explorers into the interior of this country. But the later Elvis is a very comforting figure. . . . he's very priestly; I see him almost as the Pope."

In this construct, Presley's trademark white jumpsuit becomes the Pope's vestments, and "his hair is the miter." Continuing the metaphor, Graceland—its interior done in the "Elvisian colors" of gold and red—becomes the ornately decorated Vatican. Elvis ministered to his fans like a religious leader, offering them the sweat of his brow on white silk scarves.

"And they have gift shops all over the Vatican," Chadwick says. "It's really no different from Graceland; they sell postcards with the Pope's picture on them."

•   •   •

Robert Lopez sees Aztec imagery in Elvis's jumpsuits. As El Vez, the former art gallery curator and east L.A. punk rocker offers us a "translation" of the Elvis myth, postulating a Latino Elvis with the revolutionary impulses of Che Guevara.

"Like Barry Manilow," he boasts, "I write the songs that make the world revolt."

His show is tight and good-humored, though it's clear that Elvis doesn't mean the same thing to El Vez as he does to Mark Hussman or Rick Saucedo. For El Vez, Elvis isn't so much a role to inhabit as an icon to subvert, to bend to his own uses. He is a smart artist, playing with the role of impersonator and performer, smudging lines between homage and satire.

Take "En el Barrio," his version of "In the Ghetto," for instance. El Vez sings:

Out of East L.A.

With no more gangs and no more crime

To the promised land

Out in Anaheim

Near Disneyland

Sure, it's a funny line, but the pastiche pays attention to its source and it's socially coherent. It's almost earnest enough for Elvis. Of course, it helps that—with the Memphis Mariachis—El Vez has a hot band.

"I think of Robert as an especially smart graduate student," Chadwick says, noting that he's already extended—and El Vez has accepted—an offer to come back to the second International Conference of Elvis Presley to lecture. "I talked to him as an equal. He has a great understanding of what he's doing; I told him he was doing the same thing on stage that I was trying to do in the classroom."

Robert Lopez got into the Elvis business almost by accident; he became interested in the phenomenon after overseeing a kitschy Elvis memorabilia show at *La Luz de Jesus* in Los Angeles five years ago. Immersion in Presleyania for a month led him to fly to Memphis during Weep Week, rewriting some of Elvis's lyrics on the plane. He landed, then did a set outside Graceland in gold lamé pants and a matching sombrero. And the shtick took—though he thought it was a one-shot, El Vez has been paying his bills.

"I do other stuff, too," Lopez/El Vez says, "but I genuinely love Elvis. He typifies the American Dream—to everyone. You don't have be a revolutionary. When I was a kid I saw Elvis wearing continental slacks and slicked-back hair—he looked like my uncles."

> Elvis was a hero to most
> But he never meant shit to me you see
> Straight up racist that sucker was
> Simple and plain
> Mother fuck him and John Wayne.
>
> —Public Enemy,
> "Fight the Power"

Universal Elvis. Elvis is, as Mojo Nixon tells us, everywhere. He's no respecter of race or gender or nationality. The Chinese Elvis lives in Chicago and wears cheap chrome sunglasses he bought in a Graceland gift shop. White Trash cracker Elvis Paul MacLeod turned his Holly Springs house into a frightening museum.

Howard Finster, the folk artist, probably spoke to him last week. All that's believable. So why not Charlie Feathers's theory?

A few years ago, in a rockabilly fanzine called *The Bob*, Feathers, a minor rockabilly god who knew Elvis in Memphis when both were recording at Sun Studios, claimed that Elvis's father was black.

"His hair was always wet and slicked down, 'cause the minute it dried everybody'd know," Feathers said. "Yes sir, he dyed his eyebrows and eyelashes too. Not too many people know it, but Gladys took a trip to Florida without Vernon and was carryin' on with a colored fella down there and was pregnant right after. Nope, Vernon ain't his daddy. No sir."

While there is absolutely no reason to believe Feathers's testimony—the man tells stories—it might be simpler if we could. For Elvis made the explosion and assimilation of black culture in the sixties and seventies possible—unlike Pat or Georgia Gibbs, Elvis wasn't a tamer of black music, his performances were rough—sometimes rawer than the original. In his day, Elvis was a not only a symbol of integration; in him the extremes of black and white, good and bad, sacred and profane were impossibly suspended.

In the interesting 1981 quasidocumentary *This Is Elvis*, we watch with fascination as an old central casting cracker—a real person!—announces that he and his buddies have set out to check the growth of this new jungly music:

"We've set up a 20-man committee to do away with this vulgar, animalistic, nigger rock 'n' roll bop. Our committee will check with the restaurant owners, and the cafes, to see what Presley records is on their machines, and then ask them to do away with them."

Though there are rumors that Elvis was a bigot—famously, Chuck D. of the rap group Public Enemy has claimed as much—it is difficult to believe. Elvis did not rip off black culture so much as he popularized it, gave it a foot in the door. Elvis made the cross-pollination of American culture not only possible, but inevitable; Elvis didn't invent rock 'n' roll so much as make it possible for it to take over the world.

In the strictest sense, Elvis was not a songwriter, but he was an innovator and synthesizer and—as much of the press pegged him at the time—a "cultural barbarian" unwittingly straining at the gates. Elvis wore his Lansky Brothers toreador jackets and his hair long and greasy and listened to black musicians—gospel singers back in Shake Rag in Tupelo, blues ranters in Memphis—because it was a part of him. There was no conscious attempt at appropriating black music for commercial gain; thousands of other white kids were listening to the same stuff Elvis was listening to, to Big Joe Turner and Arthur Crudup.

In a June 26, 1956, interview with a group of reporters in Charlotte, North Carolina, Presley defended his overtly sexual performances by saying, "The colored folks been singing it and playing it just like I'm doin' now, man, for more years than I know."

"They played it like that in the shanties and in their juke joints, and nobody paid it no mind till I goosed it up. I got it from them. Down in Tupelo, Mississippi, I used to hear old Arthur Crudup bang his box the way I do now, and I said if I ever got to the place where I could feel all old Arthur felt, I'd be a music man like nobody ever saw."

Elvis was poor, but he was not, his father Vernon insisted, "trash." He was not a bigot. "We never had any prejudice," Vernon once said. "We never put anybody down. Neither did Elvis."

• • •

Only moments before he collapsed, spinning—perhaps drunkenly—to the stage of the Education Auditorium, the rock critic Stanley Booth gave Dewey Phillips and Sam—the two unrelated Memphis men who played the biggest roles in shaping the teenager who would become Elvis Presley—credit for nothing less than "creating" the second half of the twentieth century.

It was the conference's finest moment.

Booth, the chronicler of the Rolling Stones and biographer of Keith Richards, swooned in the middle of his talk about the influence of gospel music on the young Elvis—he was quickly revived and his first words on coming to were "In the spirit of Elvis Presley . . . ."

(Booth was able to complete his rambling yet altogether brilliant lecture a day later, completing what Chadwick characterized as a most Elvis-like cycle of resurrection and redemption.)

His crash notwithstanding, Booth's statements about Sam and Dewey, the producer and the disc jockey—made completely without irony—cut right to the crux of the matter; the Phillips boys created the second half of the twentieth century because they, to a great extent, created Elvis, the unavoidable icon of our time.

What Elvis did, at first unconsciously and later with terrible self-consciousness, was establish the vocabulary of gestures that we now recognize as rock 'n' roll. That's not all he did, but it's a start—perhaps it is enough to give us cause to consider why there isn't at least one Southern university with a Department of Elvis Studies.

Elvis was a singer, but that's not exactly why he is important or why some folks feel he's worthy of an international confluence of academics. Pop singers dissolve with the passing of their moment; Elvis has become an American icon as recognizable as Mickey Mouse or Coca Cola.

Indeed, the further away we get from the historic Elvis, the boy from Tupelo who cut some sides for Sam Phillips at Sun Studios, who fell asleep at night listening to Sister Rosetta Tharpe on Dewey Phillips's radio show on WHBQ on Gayosa Street in Memphis, Tennessee, the longer his shadow grows.

We all have our own Elvis, our own hot glowing knowledge of what he means. Here at the conference, his portrait hangs Mao-like behind each speaker; his power is channeled through a VCR and projected on the big screen. He snarls, he curls his lip and grinds his hips, burlesquing his own Elvishood. He speaks to you, he speaks to me, but maybe he's not saying the same thing. Is this the white boy who could sound black who'd make Sam Phillips a millionaire? The simple country kid who wielded politeness as a shield for his own throbbing insecurity? Maybe your Elvis is the fat man tucked and zipped into a white leather jumpsuit, defusing every potentially dangerous—every potentially authentic—moment with soft mumbled drawl and a kitschy karate kick?

But Elvis wasn't/isn't Frankenstein, stitched together from old parts and animated by a couple of mad scientists named Phillips. Elvis may not have been an artist, or rather he may have been—as the Rev. Howard Finster suggests—a self-taught folk artist incapable of expressing in intellectual terms his own heart's desires and appetites. Elvis was an amazingly good singer, he was young and white and handsome, and Sam Phillips believed he could apply his formula to any kid with a passable voice and the proper attitude. He thought he could duplicate Elvis's success—and he almost did with Carl Perkins, Johnny Cash, and Jerry Lee Lewis—and that's why he let Elvis go to RCA.

But while Sam Phillips loosed something in Elvis, it was already thumping in his chest.

• • •

There are those who want their Elvis divided into spheres, into Good Elvis and Bad Elvis, into the "authentic" and the "kitsch." They want the Elvis of '56 and the Elvis of '68, and they want to ignore the bloated corpse on the toilet.

All right. Maybe that's a fair thing to do, to remember Elvis as lean and surly, as Gladys's boy, as the Hillbilly Cat, while dismissing the later Elvis, the karate-kicking, pill-gobbling, talent-squandering "entertainer" who ended up lonely and bored and flooded by television light in Graceland.

Because Elvis wasn't Elvis at the end, man, not even close. Elvis wasn't Elvis when he made those movies; Elvis wasn't Elvis when he sang those stupid stupid songs. But he was.

John Shelton Reed, a professor of Southern Studies at the University of North Carolina and a culturally conservative essayist on all things Southern, tells us that Elvis was so ordinary in his beginnings as to typify a certain kind of hardscrabble Southern existence.

"There were hundreds of thousands of white Southern boys just like Elvis all throughout the region," Reed insists—working-class fodder for the new factories of the New South. He got his first guitar only because Gladys would not let him have a .22 rifle; he sang the Red Sovine song "Ol Shep" at the Alabama-Mississippi State Fair in Tupelo when he was ten years old. In his high school yearbook, he looks ordinary, almost ugly; his face is forgettable, the face of a pump jockey back when they had those kinds of jobs.

Gene Smith, Elvis's cousin and constant companion in the early years, appears at the conference to remind us of what Elvis might have been without the Elvishood. A calm, sturdy man with a sense of humor about himself. A redneck *mensch*.

• • •

Elvis was a redneck, and so is Will Campbell, a Baptist minister, civil rights activist, performer, and self-described "writer of rare books" from Mt. Juliet, Tennessee. In an impassioned rant against Yankee elitism, Campbell railed against American society's inherent distrust and proclivity to dismiss all things Southern and rural. Campbell saw in Elvis and the Southern Tenant Farmers' Union an effort to galvanize poor Southern whites and blacks—to make them realize how much they had in common despite the rift between them that had been promoted for decades by an elite white power structure.

Campbell tells how Elvis, like the quickly suppressed biracial farmers' union of the depression, both "sought to heal the rift" and make poor blacks and whites realize they shared "the same pain, the same maltreatment and exploitation, the same enemy that continues to promote the cleft between them for political and economic gain."

But even El Vez knows that Elvis was more Charro than Che.

And while the conference provided moments both surreal and genuinely provoking, it didn't begin to explain Elvis. So they'll have another one next year, and maybe one after that, and maybe it will continue to grow. Despite the mayor's objections, it could only help the city; and the side trips to Tupelo and Memphis—to the tourist spots—do no real harm.

A visitor in Oxford the Saturday before the conference opened noticed a T-shirt that read: "Dig up the fat boy."

That's what we did; we pulled him up out of the ground and clattered his bones, carved out our own charms.

Having signed over his career to the high-rolling Col. Tom Parker at its outset, Elvis was neither prepared nor particularly interested in making decisions of artistic consequence. Elvis was an arrested adolescent—he never bothered to take responsibility for his career; it was absolutely beyond him. Elvis was a shy Memphis kid who had trouble playing his guitar and singing for the musicians who gathered for his first recording session. He got lucky.

And he knew it. He spent his life waiting for it to blow away.

I think this surmised feeling of inferiority and lack of faith in his own talent might explain why one of the finest singers of the century was reduced to recording some of the silliest songs ("Song of the Shrimp," "No Room to Rumba in a Sports Car") ever committed to vinyl.

Elvis is the greatest tragedy of rock 'n' roll, for his is the greatest talent ever squandered. Elvis was a rocker in style only. His heart and mind—apparent in his vulgar, glittery tastes— were low bourgeois. He would have no truck with Kerouac or Pollack; he held no pretensions to artistry—no aspiration—he was interested only in popular acceptance as manifested in hit records and dispensable Cadillacs. It is hard to argue that he betrayed the tradition, since there was no tradition with which to keep faith.

But he wasn't a cipher, he wasn't a fool. He was a genius, some kind of way. And now he's our own saint.

Vernon Chadwick compares Elvis to those classic Greek heroes, you know, Achilles and all them. He's got that fatal flaw, that nick of imperfection that makes us empathize with him. I think that's kinda right.

I wouldn't say this conference isn't kind of a scam, because it is in a way. But not in a bad way. It's like Duke's gig—not the real thing, not even an incredible simulation, but genuinely useful.

It is a shame most people who proclaim their undying devotion to Elvis almost always miss the fundamental point of his career—insulation and power are corrosive and megastardom is a peculiar circle of hell. Michael Jackson, to name the most obvious example, could benefit from Elvis's example.

Even an incredible talent must work to keep some connection to his or her audience. Or else the audience will go crazy trying to claw through to the star.

Maybe that's why we ought to search for Elvis, because he retreated from the world, drew up like Howard Hughes, became a joke—the model for his son-in-law's tragic career. We look for Elvis because he left the building way too early, before the third act. We look for Elvis because he's gone, because he left us looking nothing like he was—a rich man sprawling on a bathroom floor, a spray of candy-colored pills around his heavy corpse.

Unlike Stanley Booth, nobody heard him fall; nobody came to help. Those last years in Graceland were long, filled with boredom and—I'm guessing—a kind of inexpressible rage.

Where is Elvis?

Everywhere. The world's popular culture is shot through with Elvisness—the King's musk is on everything from the jeans we wear to the television we watch. Elvis is a Rorschach test; like the Bible, he can be made to stand for any number of conceits, ideas, and dreams. In Elvis, one can find validation for all sorts of theories about the trembling of the heart and the rocking of the world.

He's one of us; he's one with us.

(1995)

CeDell Davis

Tender grass blooms in the mud beside a warped and weathered plywood ramp. The ramp, for his wheelchair, rises a few inches to meet a concrete slab and gives away the location of CeDell Davis's apartment in Pine Bluff, Arkansas.

It is a lucky thing, for there are more than twenty identical buildings in this complex, all flat-roofed and cinder-blocked and painted a sickly pale yellow. In compensation for the grim suburban chill, the streets all bear the prefix "Wood"; there is a "Woodlea" and a "Woodbine" and a "Woodlawn." At least the residents of this drear place have the comfort of a fine address.

This seems an unlikely harbor of genius, but Davis is a bluesman, and the blues requires the endurance of hardship. Inside his small apartment, with its linoleum floor and ever-burning console color television, he sits and smiles. Robert Palmer, the music critic who last year produced Davis's first album, sees something "Buddha-like" in his serenity. He is sixty-six years old and just beginning to be appreciated by people who care about the idiom. His hands are gnarled into cruel hooks, and his legs are too weak to hold his weight. Still, this beatific man with hooded eyes and a suggestion of a mustache beams with intelligence and preternatural good will.

It is problematic to talk about the blues these days. Blues is a shadowy territory of uncertain boundaries and ineffable depths. Langston Hughes, the poet, once complained that white folks had taken his blues and "fixed them so they don't sound like me."

In Memphis, they've turned Beale Street into a theme park, where show bands tend the blues like hot-house flowers, unable to survive a trip down the street before melting into the urban blare of rock and rap and radio-ready country music. Here the blues are for tourists. On any night in Chicago, there might be a dozen clubs where big electrified blues get played, loud and sweaty, with the bass thrilling in your chest. This is city blues, done up like Jake and Elwood in skinny ties and Ray-Ban sunglasses (model 5022)—blues conjoined with rhythm. In New Orleans, the blues is tinged with jazz; in Austin, cowboy music creeps in. East Texas has its own strain, flowing from Blind Lemon Jefferson's needle-neat acoustic flourishes and bottom-of-the-ocean howls through T-Bone Walker's elegant electric glissando to the doomed, bent-note shriekback of Stevie Ray Vaughn.

And, of course, the Delta, with the Mississippi River running like a scar through its alluvial flatness, is the fertile crescent which birthed the blues. W. C. Handy first heard "the weird music" in Tutwiler, Mississippi, an hour southeast of Helena, in 1903, and this is the vein in which CeDell Davis and precious few others work, the *Deep Blues* Palmer wrote about in his 1981 book, documented on film and captured on record.

Deep Blues the film, which made the rounds of art theaters last year, to be released on videotape, and *Deep Blues* the album, released on Atlantic Records in 1992, document in unadorned detail the indigenous blues of the Delta, solo vocalists with electric guitars and small amps to blustering, hard-swinging ensembles. While high-profile artists like Robert Cray and Buddy Guy keep the rocking twelve-bar style alive—selling steadily and charting occasionally—only aficionados are aware of the still-extant Delta scene.

Palmer contends that the blues is not moribund. Artists such as Junior Kimbrough, R. L. Burnside, Roosevelt "Booba" Barnes, Big Jack Johnson, Jessie Mae Hemphill, and thirty-six-year-old Lonnie Pitchford are not only preserving the tradition but pushing it forward. While for years they've toiled in relative obscurity, playing silver-wooded tonks and house parties in their hometowns, and only occasionally landing a spot on the bill at a blues festival, Palmer and others have begun to record and market their music.

At the vanguard of this quiet renaissance is CeDell Davis, whose first album snuck onto some critics' top-ten lists and is selling well for Fat Possum Records, the small label that signed him to a five-album deal last year. Though Davis has appeared on a few anthology albums, and served as a sideman for Elmore James on a few early sides, *Feel Like Doin' Something Wrong* is his first "shot at the big time."

"Recording was just something I guess I never got around

to," he says. "I'm still kickin' the blues pretty good, but I'm not as fast as I once was. I can play like I used to. I still play pretty good, but I used to be scary. I mean, I was playing with all these men—Robert Nighthawk, Elmore James, Muddy Waters—when I was a boy."

While musicologists and ethnographers might describe the blues as simple music delivered in an emotionally charged style, based on a pentatonic scale with flatted thirds, fifths, and sometimes sevenths, it seems more useful to accept Davis's dictum: "So long as there is women, there will be the blues."

Davis laughs when he says this, but he means it. "If you're happy, you hear the blues and it makes you more happy," he says. "And if you're feeling bad, well the blues will make you go lower, in the other direction. Now the blues isn't about being sad, it's about feeling."

• • •

Ellis "CeDell" Davis was born in Helena, Arkansas, on June 9, 1927, when Babe Ruth was almost halfway to sixty home runs and Robert Johnson still had eleven years to walk the earth. At the time, Helena was a booming cotton port that boasted nearly a hundred juke joints and nightclubs, as well as dozens of street musicians who played well into the evening.

Davis split his time between Helena, where his parents ran a small cafe, and the E. M. Hood plantation in Clayton, Mississippi, about eight miles south of Tunica, where his older brother lived.

It was there that he and Isaiah Ross, a boyhood friend who was later to record for Sam Phillips as "Dr. Ross the Harmonica Boss," began to play around with first harmonica and then the guitar. Davis began to display some proficiency with the instrument when polio struck.

"I was nine years old when they took me to the Children's Hospital in Little Rock," he says. "I stayed there for two years and seven months."

Toward the end of his stay, he was able to buy, for two dollars, a "Buck Jones Silvertone guitar" from a fellow patient. "He was about to leave and he had two guitars, so he was happy for me to get it," Davis says. But polio had twisted his hands into cruel claws, making it impossible for him to play right-handed, the way he had learned.

So Davis flipped the instrument upside down, so that the bass strings were at the bottom. He fretted it with a butter knife held gingerly in his right hand, while raking his left across the strings. To compensate for his inability to depress given strings to make conventional chord forms, Davis developed a tuning based on, but not exactly like, the open chord tuning used by slide guitarists. He was, he says, finding a way to reproduce the sounds he heard in his own head.

"Lot of people can't play with me," he says. "You got a guitar and you get it tuned, well, you play in a certain way. You don't have to be able to hear all that well, long as you know where to put your fingers. But you play with me, you have to be able to hear that I doing it not like it usually is. Lot of people can't follow me."

On the liner notes to Davis's album, *Feel Like Doin' Something Wrong*, Palmer puts it this way:

> The knife-handle on the strings produces uneven pressure, which results in a welter of metal-stress harmonic transients and a singular tonal plasticity. Some people who hear CeDell playing for the first time think it's out of tune, but it would be more accurate to say he plays in an alternative tuning. Because the way he plays and hears chords is consistent and systematic.

Davis says it took about three years for him to regain his prowess on the guitar. And by the time he was twelve years old, he was playing "for money" in Helena and in Mississippi. "They wouldn't let me because I was underage," he says. "But they let me sit in front of the store or the bar and play because people liked my music. And then, they let me in, but they wouldn't let me mix with anybody, just sit on a cane-bottom chair and play. I was 16, 17 years old before they just let me come in a place and play."

Despite his unorthodox technique, Davis, like nearly all blues musicians, was required to perform as kind of a human jukebox, handling requests for material as diverse as Bing Crosby and Tommy Dorsey.

"I didn't even think about writing my own songs," he says. "Back then, they had a record out that people liked, you had to know how to play it, else you wouldn't get no jobs. I played what the people wanted to hear, not what I liked. That what everybody had to do."

And, though Davis today seems as "hard" and raw as any blues singer since Howlin' Wolf, he says his personal tastes ran to the more sophisticated recordings of T-Bone Walker and Big Bill Broonzy.

"I heard Robert Johnson, and I tried to play like Robert Johnson, but I couldn't really do it," he says. "I had to do what I had to do, make my own style, I guess, even though I was playing other people's songs. Do 'em my own way. I just wanted to be a blues player."

Palmer points out that Davis was playing in "some of the world's most dangerous dives," where physical violence was commonplace. Robert Johnson, the most influential blues artist of all time, died after being served an "ice course," a glass of whiskey laced with poison, in a tonk near Greenwood, Mississippi, in 1938. He was twenty-seven years old.

"It was kind of rough sometimes," Davis admits. "But I didn't think much about that. I was happy to play."

Around 1953, Davis moved to St. Louis and began an association with Robert Lee McCoy, a blues guitarist and vocalist who performed under the name "Robert Nighthawk." For about ten years the two men played together in clubs around the area, trading off lead guitar parts and "bassing," while sharing vocals. But while Nighthawk made his reputation as a great slide guitar player largely through his recording, Davis never made the trip to the studio.

"I kept askin' him when he was going to take me up to Chicago," Davis says. "He just shake his head and say there wasn't anything to recording, that he was doing better—making more money—playing around home. He didn't think it was any big deal."

In late 1957, Davis was playing a St. Louis nightclub when a police raid panicked the crowd. They swarmed over Davis, who then could walk only with crutches, breaking his legs in several places. Since then, he has been confined to a wheelchair.

"I came home to Helena on June 5, 1961," he says. "Then I got a steady date at the Jack Rabbit Club in Pine Bluff. That turned into the Jungle Hut a few years later, and I kept playing there."

Robert Palmer ran into Davis in a Clarksdale club in 1982 and arranged for him to play at Tramps Nightclub in New York City. "I played three times a week, and made $500 a night," he says. "And the people just loved me, they never heard anything like it."

•　　•　　•

In late December, Davis traveled to Atlanta to play a New Year's Eve date with the avant-garde rock outfit Colonel Bruce Hampton and the Aquarium Rescue Unit. While he was there, he cut some tracks with the band.

"Wait until you hear that," he smiles. "That was something. Now their lead guitar player, he couldn't play with me, but Bruce, he understood. He could fit in here and there. That was some wild stuff."

There is no place in Pine Bluff where Davis can play these days. The Jungle Hut closed up long ago, and other live music venues don't book blues artists. Davis can't think of a single record shop in town where his record is for sale.

"Sometimes I think about moving," he says, "but I'm here for good, I'm too old."

Davis mentions that his friend, Isaiah Ross, died last year.

"October 21," he says softly. "He was a good one."

Ross played guitar left-handed, with the strings strung upside down just like Davis. He worked building General Motors cars in Flint, Michigan, for thirty-seven years, and when he suffered the heart attack he was never to recover from, they had to literally carry him out of the plant.

"It always been music with me," Davis says. "Even though it seems like it's just beginning to happen for me, I was in my 50s before I ever saw what I could do. But I happy. It's kind of like Satchel Paige. He was old and slow before he got anyone to pay attention."

And Davis didn't find that he had an aptitude for writing his own songs until the past few years. Now he's always scribbling verses, holding onto them for the time he'll set them to music. Now he has the time to write and dream.

"I always wanted to be the kind of person that people remember," he says. "Not someone who get buried, then fifteen minutes later nobody knows who they were. I always wanted to leave something behind, something that would go on and on."

He pauses.

"I get the feeling I'm going leave something behind, one way or the other. There's a lot of good blues been lost, but as long as there's people, there's going to be blues."

(1994)

Mr. Petty's Case

*"I think I'm a little more—dare I say—
eccentric than Springsteen and Bob Seger."*

—Tom Petty,
Playback liner notes

When you start to talk about Tom Petty and how he fits into our cultural landscape, you've got to go back a bit. Because Tom Petty has been around a while, and because he is so easy to take for granted. Start reeling off the names of the American rock 'n' roll heroes—the real deal guys, starting with Chuck Berry and Elvis—and it may take you a while to get to the lanky Floridian with the cornsilk hair.

People like Tom Petty; they like the expansive jangle and grace of his singles, but they don't necessarily consider him "an important artist." He's not Bruce Springsteen singing about the socioeconomic consequences inherent in the paradigm shift from industrial to service economies. He's not Bob Dylan muttering mad prayers. He works a vein of mainstream pop, singing mostly about girls.

So if one were going to make a case for Petty and his Heartbreakers as the preeminent American rock 'n' roll band of their time, if one were to suggest that maybe the Heartbreakers are the direct descendants of Creedence Clearwater Revival or simply the American equivalent of the Rolling Stones—if you don't like T.P. you simply don't like rock 'n' roll—one had better prepare.

MCA has helped, with the release of *Playback,* a ninety-two-track, six-CD retrospective of Petty's career from 1973 (when he left Gainesville, Florida, for Los Angeles) through 1993 (when he signed with Warner Brothers). It helps to hear all the music laid end to end, to note the remarkable consistency and the quirks, to hear something like an evolution of his sound. One can be overwhelmed by the sheer bulk of the material; there are three discs full of hits and should-have-been hits, balanced by another three discs of B-sides, rarities, and demos.

There is an eighty-three-page booklet with a historical essay by veteran rock journalist Bill Flanagan that frankly describes the band's drug problems, internal squabbling, and the "dark period" in the mid eighties. In addition to this useful mini-biography, there are track-by-track notes featuring the comments of Petty and his bandmates. And so we learn that "Listen to Her Heart" was written after Petty's wife, Jane, "went to Ike Turner's house and got locked in" and that Petty was miffed when Stevie Nick's record company timed the release of "Stop Draggin My Heart Around" (featuring Tom Petty and the Heartbreakers) to coincide with the release of Petty's own "A Woman in Love" single.

Priced at around seventy dollars the box set is not likely to sell millions, but for the serious fan, it is an all but essential artifact. There isn't a track on the compilation that seems super-fluous; even the studio outtake "Moon Pie" is, in context, illuminating. All the pieces are there, the career itself convinces. It's all there—as they used to say when vinyl was the common currency—in the grooves.

● ● ●

To understand and fully appreciate Tom Petty, one must understand that rock 'n' roll—as opposed to the corporatized "rock"—is essentially a Southern thing.

Whether it's Jersey boy Springsteen affecting the beaten vowels of the sharecropper, sir, or Britishers Mick and Keef droppin' their "g's" or even Dylan—the boy from the North Country —trying to sound like Blind Willie McTell, the inflections of rock 'n' roll have always been Southern.

Rock 'n' roll might belong to anyone who wants it bad enough, but you have to acknowledge that it started here, below America's belt—Elvis and Little Richard and Jerry Lee Lewis and Carl Perkins and Ike Turner and Sam Phillips and Dewey Phillips and all those wild Burnett boys who started the grass fire that would consume the world. Rock 'n' roll is a Southern thing—always has been.

But there is also such a thing as Southern Rock. It's over now; it flashed across the empty skies of the seventies and was gone. It was beautiful to watch, but Southern rock was a shooting star, not a fixed planet.

It was provincial and reactionary, a stubborn regional sound with thuggish fans who didn't for a minute buy into any of that hippie-dippy peace and love junk. It was a kind of "know-nothing" music, redneck rock that wrapped itself in the Stars 'n' Bars as well as in Old Glory.

It could be dumb music; sometimes it celebrated getting drunk or getting stoned or getting in a fight or getting a gun. Sometimes it dealt in stereotypes; sometimes it encouraged mindless rowdyism as the answer to systematic exclusion from full economic participation in America.

Sometimes, though, it was better than that; sometimes it offered up the concerns and attitudes of ordinary working-class folks as well as any form of pop expression; sometimes—as when the clean lines of Duane Allman's and Dickey Bett's Gibson guitars snaked around each other, when brother Gregg's bluesy voice began to ripen and roar—Southern rock could be majestic, lyrical and sweet and beyond interpretation.

And while it's over—it ended violently, amid the torn rubber and twisted steel of various motorcycle and plane crashes—it isn't quite dead. Southern rock flickers on in the passing phrases of guitar bands like REM, even in the full-throated bellow of a "modern rock" singer like Eddie Vedder.

Perhaps the major revelation of *Playback* is that Tom Petty and the Heartbreakers are a Southern band—not just a band from the South.

When they first surfaced as a national act in 1976, it was easy to see the Heartbreakers as a "new wave" act, with their economical singles and emotional urgency. At the time songs such as the Byrds-like "American Girl" and the Stones-ish "Breakdown" seemed more a reaction to the bloated, faceless corporate competence of bands like Journey and Styx than a continuation—and advancement—of the mainstream pop tradition.

No wonder the Heartbreakers were booked with bands like the Ramones and Blondie; no wonder that high school punk rockers were working out versions of "I Need to Know" and "Refugee."

"It would have been real easy to say . . . we are new wave and get the skinny ties," Petty once told writer Dave Marsh. "But it never looked like much of a challenge to me. It looked like a bigger challenge to work in the mainstream, to play to everybody. I never understood being so cool that nobody heard it."

•   •   •

Beneath Petty's most obvious influences—both his ringing Rickenbacker twelve-string and his nasal upper register are ringers for the Byrds Roger McGuinn—lurk the bluesy grit and clean, muscular lines of the Allmans and Lynyrd Skynyrd. (We learn from the *Playback* liner notes that Mudcrutch, Petty's first band, occasionally shared the bill with the pre-fame Skynyrd in Gainesville bars.)

Perhaps the most telling track on the set is a live cover of Charlie Rich's rockabilly classic "Lonely Weekends" that ties the whole rock 'n' roll-blues-country package up nicely; there's no question that Petty and his band inhabit this music. If his voice can't quite pull off Jimmy Reed-style menace on his cover of "Big Boss Man," it's supple enough to goof on Elvis ("Baby, Let's Play House," "Wooden Heart," and "G.I. Blues") or to pay homage to Solomon Burke ("Cry to Me").

Of course, Petty's Southerness has not prevented him from incorporating other styles into his music. While basically a rock 'n' roll fundamentalist who turns to the Byrds (and through them to their antecedents, Dylan and Nashville) for melodic elegance and to the Stones for power, Petty has enjoyed a fruitful collaboration with Eurythmics' techno-guitarist Dave Stewart ("Don't Come Around Here No More") and Jeff Lynne, the former guiding light of Electric Light Orchestra turned Beatlesque producer.

Lynne—whose most recent high-profile project was helping the remaining Beatles assemble that dubious "Free as a Bird" single around an old, unfinished John Lennon demo—worked with Petty on "Full Moon Fever," his first solo album, and with Petty and the Heartbreakers on "Into the Great Wide Open."

Petty's openness to new approaches has helped his music retain a certain freshness; though it no doubt helps that he writes economical, punchy pop songs that sound timeless.

While it comes as no surprise to those who've paid more than cursory attention to his career—especially not to those who've seen them play live—*Playback* also emphasizes that Tom Petty and the Heartbreakers is in fact a band rather than a singer/songwriter backed by sure but secondary musicians.

While Petty is certainly the group's guiding intelligence, both co-writer and guitarist Mike Campbell and keyboard player Benmont Tench contribute essential elements to the Heartbreakers' sound. While—like Keith Richards, the player he most resembles—the instinctive, inventive Campbell works blues scales almost exclusively, he seems immune to self-indulgent lead guitarist tendencies.

Tench's playing is reminiscent both of Dylan's *Blonde on Blonde* period and of Alan Price's work with the Animals, adding a highly identifiable gospel tinge to the band's work.

For more than twenty years, Petty and the Heartbreakers have been amazingly reliable—both in commercial terms and artistic quality. There have been no obvious false steps and, even now, none of the early songs sound anachronistic. While his name may not be the first that comes to mind when one starts talking about the bonafide, first-tier rock 'n' roll pantheon; perhaps it shouldn't be too far down the list. Presley, Dylan, Springsteen, Berry, . . . Petty?

Petty has outdone most of his influences—his legacy is likely to outlast that of the Byrds, or the Allman Brothers, or Lynyrd Skynyrd. He has always been there, grinning, his horsey face amused by fashion, always ready to play but never to give in.

(1996)

Always Patsy Cline

Recently, a record album by a comely young singer named Shania Twain replaced Patsy Cline's *Greatest Hits* as the all-time best-selling record by a female country artist. That's quite an accomplishment for Ms. Twain; congratulations are in order. However harshly the critics judge her—and there have been some lukewarm reviews—she is in the business of selling records, and she's done that very well. In a relatively short period, she's enjoyed remarkable success.

Yet Shania Twain is really nothing more than a pop phenomenon—another girl country singer who's managed to cross over and catch the public imagination. Much of her success is due to the persona her record company and publicists have crafted; however professional her sound, however well she understands her material, the greater part of the creature called Shania Twain—of any nineties pop star—are the images that flicker on television tubes, that glow in fan magazines and shimmer in plastic jewel cases. Talent is an ingredient, a necessary component, but only part—the lesser part—of the package.

It was different with Patsy Cline.

Sure, she had the macabre advantage of dying young, in a plane crash like Buddy Holly. But that's not what people think of when they think of Patsy Cline. When we remember Patsy Cline, we don't think of the well-tempered image, the forever-young face caught in amber. We don't think of Patsy Cline as a babyfat girl singer with a woolly thatch of dark-brown hair in pedal-pushers; we think of "Crazy," "Sweet Dreams," "I Fall to Pieces," or "Walkin' after Midnight."

To most of us, Patsy Cline is less an American icon tragically frozen at the height of her powers than something much more simple.

Patsy Cline is a voice.

A devastating voice.

Patsy Cline is the real thing; there's nothing false about what she's doing—her voice, her instrument, is strong enough to overcome any triteness of arrangement. Weak songs don't stand a chance with her. Her voice is like a hurricane, an irresistible force that rips long-standing assumptions up by their roots and tosses them around like so much dandelion fluff.

You see, Patsy Cline isn't really a country singer, or even a pop singer; she is just the singer. It's really more valid to compare her to Frank Sinatra or Tony Bennett or Elvis Presley or Barbara Streisand—pop singers with the capacity for genuine vocal art—than to admittedly great country singers like Kitty Wells or Loretta Lynn or Tammy Wynette.

Patsy Cline had roots in country music—no, check that— *hillbilly* music, but in the end, she transcends all genres. People who don't like country music—not even the silky, torchy kind of country music that Patsy Cline helped create—like Patsy Cline. While she may not be selling as well as Shania Twain or Faith Hill, Cline's records are still selling, people are still listening.

• • •

While the facts of Cline's life are fairly well known—thanks largely to the 1985 movie biography *Sweet Dreams*, which featured Jessica Lange as the singer—it might help to review a few key points. For instance, "Patsy Cline" was, like Shania Twain, to some degree, a creation designed to sell records. Her real name was Virginia Patterson Hensley, and she was born in 1932 in Gore, Virginia, the daughter of a blacksmith.

By the age of four, she had taught herself to dance and had won an amateur contest in Lexington. She sang in school musicals and at community benefits and even in minstrel shows. In 1956, she told Meredith Buel of the *Washington Star* that she had discovered her ample voice after a childhood brush with death.

"You might say it was my return to the living that launched me as a singer," she said. "In childhood I developed a serious throat infection, and my heart stopped beating. I was placed in an oxygen tent, and doctors brought me back to life. I recovered from the illness with a voice that boomed like Kate Smith's."

After she guested on a traveling show hosted by *Grand Ole Opry* regular Wally Fowler in 1948, Fowler arranged for sixteen-year-old Virginia to appear on Roy Acuff's noontime *Dinner Bell* program on the Nashville radio station WSM. It looked good, but an audition for *Grand Ole Opry* impresario Jim Denny did not quite work out as she had planned. Denny failed to offer her an immediate spot on the *Opry,* and the Hensleys' finances dictated that she return to Winchester—where they had moved when Virginia was in grammar school—and resume her job as a counter girl in a drugstore.

When she was twenty, "Patsy" Hensley—she changed her name at the behest of band leader Bill Peer, with whom she worked for six years—married Gerald Cline, whose family owned a successful construction company. It was a tumultuous marriage, and it really didn't last more than a few months. Pasty later described herself as a "hellcat"—she liked to drink liquor and stay out late and so did Gerald Cline. Apparently they just didn't do that much hellraising together.

By the time Patsy Cline was ready to try Nashville again, the country music industry had undergone considerable changes. Starting in 1949, it was no longer listed as "Hillbilly" music in the pages of *Billboard.* And following the rise of Lefty Frizzell and Hank Williams (and later Elvis Presley), the focus shifted from band leaders to charismatic solo vocalists. Kitty Wells had emerged as the first major female star of country music (her signature 1952 hit "It Wasn't God Who Made Honky Tonk Angels" remains one of the most important recordings ever).

Patsy finally divorced Gerald Cline in March 1957 and married Charlie Dick six months later. At that time, despite the success of her first hit, "Walkin' after Midnight," her career seemed stalled. She wouldn't have another chart record until 1960. Then, just as things seemed to be taking off again, she died in that airplane crash in March 1963.

•　　•　　•

Indeed, Patsy Cline never had a million-selling record during her lifetime. She was never as big a star as her contemporaries Brenda Lee and Connie Francis. Only posthumously does she seem to be as big as she in fact was. She was great.

Everyone knows—or ought to know—about her work with legendary producer Owen Bradley. Together they crafted songs that were more pop than country, songs that used strings and cocktail pianos and rockabilly guitars behind that elemental voice. Records that hold up.

Listen to one of her more obscure, one of her slightest records, something like "I Love You, Honey" from early 1956. It is an obvious song, a lightweight honky-tonk boogie number with a fiddle introduction and a guitar line that might have been played by someone who might be imitating Scotty Moore (it might be the great Grady Marti; if so it's one of his weakest performances). Eddie Miller, who wrote the song (and the classic "Release Me"), later claimed it was the first song he ever wrote— at age fourteen. It sounds like it.

"I Love You, Honey" is a period piece, hopelessly dated.

Except for the vocal.

Cline's performance is flip and offhand, a bit brassy, but full and finally convincing. She doesn't throw away the song with the commercial jingle treatment it deserves, neither does she bear down too hard, trying to milk blood from this turnip. Instead she glides through it, riding just ahead of the beat, occasionally allowing her voice to catch something of the quality of ripping silk: *"I love you, honey / I love your money / But most of all I love your automobile . . ."*

It's a revelation—straw spun into almost gold. She's that much better than the song.

So it's no wonder that when fitted with good material— Willie Nelson's "Crazy," Don Hecht's "Walkin' after Midnight,"— Cline produced records that cut across boundaries, records that can't be sorted into genres.

Patsy Cline wasn't rock or pop or country; she was more than any radio airplay format. She was Patsy Cline. And, even when the material didn't match her talent, she was always Patsy Cline.

(1996)

Dylan's Children (and Everybody's)

"You got to be somewhat superstitious to survive. People like to talk about the new image of America but to me it's still the old one—Marlon Brando, James Dean, Marilyn Monroe, it's not computers, cocaine and David Letterman, we gotta get off that—Hedy Lamarr, Dorothy Danridge, that's my idea of America . . . who's improved on it?"

—Bob Dylan,
notes for *Biograph*

Once, in the 1980s, at a party in Morningside Heights, not far from Columbia University, an N.Y.U. film student pointed out Bob Dylan's daughter to a friend. Would you like to be introduced? the film student asked; his friend declined. Dylan's daughter looked like she was having fun, like she might have forgotten for the moment she was Dylan's daughter. It was better to leave her alone; she looked happy.

All Dylan's children have a special burden; their famous father was famous in part for hiding them out, for having shielded them from the pop of flash bulbs, the hot stare of klieg lights, the killing fallout of celebrity. The film student's friend figured it would be, if not rude, at least inappropriate to make Dylan's daughter's acquaintance; knowing that she was Dylan's daughter poisoned all possibilities of human interaction. Maybe, he thought, if you simply met Dylan's daughter, and only later found out who her father was, it might be OK; then there might be a chance you wouldn't send her spinning off in horror, crashing down the stairs and into the cold, brittle, merciless New York night. Maybe.

It must be tough being Dylan's kid.

Dylan himself would know, if you could locate him to ask him. Because Dylan created Dylan, he thought him up and gave

him his name and his history. Robert Zimmerman was someone else, a personality subsumed by his own willful creation, by
the monster he made of himself. Say the name comes from
Dylan Thomas, the Bushmills-soaked poet, and Dylan will deny
it, sometimes. At least he has, on occasion, denied it.

Nothing is for certain about this Dylan, and while the facts
of Zimmerman's existence are ascertainable, they reveal virtually
nothing about the kid.

Like Dizzy Dean and Satchel Paige, Dylan/Zimmerman told
stories to entertain and to obscure, to cover the tracks that led
out of the Minnesota Iron Range. In the early days, he would tell
folks he was an orphan—and then fifteen years later he had his
mom, Beatty Zimmerman, on stage with him during the Rolling
Thunder Revue.

But, Nat Hentoff tells us, when Joan Baez tried to dance
Dylan's mom down to the principal microphone to sing a cho-
rus of Woody Guthrie's "This Land Is Your Land," Dylan kicked
Joanie—the girl on the half-shell—gently in her behind. Dylan
wasn't willing to give up the spotlight to Mrs. Zimmerman.

You might think it was Woody Guthrie in the beginning,
but it wasn't. First it was Johnny Ray, Hank Snow, and Hank
Williams and the illicit late-night rhythm and blues that sailed
in from Chicago—Jimmy Reed, John Lee Hooker, and Howlin'
Wolf. Little Zimmie—Dylan himself said we could call him that,
in "Gotta Serve Somebody"—played in a few teenage bands,
The Golden Chords, Elston Gunn & The Rock Boppers, showed
up for a high school talent show with a credible impersonation
of Little Richard.

His favorite singer was Bobby Vee; he liked Elvis and Marlon
Brando and leather jackets and motorcycles.

He got the hell out of Hibbing, Minnesota, away from that
dim doomed midwestern mining town, stopped off at the
University of Minnesota, joined a frat, and ended up playing
folk music in a little club called the 10 O'Clock Scholar in a
place they called Dinkytown. He learned a trade. He took off for
Madison, Wisconsin, then to Chicago for a few months, and
finally on to New York.

Maybe you know the rest, the adventures in Greenwich
Village, the session where he played harmonica for Harry
Belafonte, the review by Robert Shelton in the *New York Times*

(". . . there is no doubt he is bursting at the seams with talent," Shelton wrote about a Dylan performance at Gerde's Folk City, an unprecedented event since Dylan was only the show's opening act, not the headliner), and the way he was signed by Columbia Records producer and talent scout John Hammond—the man who "discovered" Bessie Smith, Aretha Franklin, Billie Holiday, and later Bruce Springsteen.

Maybe you know how the first album was released just before the singer turned twenty-one, that it sold miserably and was dubbed "Hammond's Folly." Maybe you know it contained only one song written by Dylan himself, the shakily derivative "Song to Woody."

It was "Blowin' in the Wind," off the second album, that was published in *Broadside* magazine in 1962; it was subsequently recorded by Peter, Paul and Mary and became the fastest-selling single in Warner Brothers history.

Dylan became a darling of the folk crowd. Then he went electric and got booed, and emerged as a rock hero. He had a spooky James Dean–like motorcycle accident, his marriage broke up, he became "born again." If you don't know the history, you could look it up or watch it on TV.

●　　●　　●

There is a scene in *Don't Look Back,* the D. A. Pennebaker film of Dylan's 1965 tour of England. Backstage, before a concert in Newcastle, a young blond man with fat glasses approaches Dylan and sidekick Bob Neuwirth. Awed by the scruffy twenty-four-year-old musician, this "science student" obviously wants to scrape up against Dylan, to make some kind of connection to the artist.

After a few minutes of painful teasing—a cat batting a mouse between its paws—Dylan lunges for the student's throat.

"I'm—I'm a person, you know," the wounded student pleads.

"Well, so what? There's a million, thousand, billion—there's so many people outside. Only you can't know them all."

"No, no, but ah—ah, if I meet somebody, ah, to speak to them a few minutes, I think that guy might be able to give me something."

"Well, now we're getting down there, huh? What is it that you want?"

"Um, everyone is out for whatever they can get. Well, I might be able to get—I might be able to get something material."

"You might be able to get a chick!"

A second later, a disgusted Neuwirth hands the science student an old harmonica. He protests that he doesn't want it, that he can't play it—but it's all he gets and maybe more than he deserves.

•   •   •

Thirty years on, our Dylan is still a crank. You might not like him as a person, and he might not like you. So what?

You get what you get from him and not much else. You get the music, and though some people don't *get* the music, it's really all that is available.

He is an artist that demands a lot from his children, from those of us who've alternately embraced and rejected him over the years. He is prickly, wheezy, squinting, and difficult. One of the most closely guarded secrets at Columbia during the 1960s was how small Dylan's album sales actually were—they even let him slip away during the early 1970s, to record *Planet Waves* on Asylum. It was only a few years ago that his debut album finally sold enough to be certified as a gold record. And he's not playing before tens of thousands in stadiums, like the Rolling Stones; he's playing small halls and auditoriums.

There are a lot of people who don't like Dylan, who say he is not musical, that he can't sing, that his concerts have become tedious.

While it's OK to not like Dylan—there are interesting people who, for whatever reason, simply do not *get* Dylan—it is just wrong to say he is unmusical. He is a gifted guitar player (listen to his first album or the recent *World Gone Wrong*), and he is a much better singer than he lets on (listen to "Percy's Song" off the *Biograph* collection or to "Lay Lady Lay"). Technically, his harmonica playing may be suspect, but technically, John Lennon was a lousy musician; he makes a gorgeous groaning noise.

When he wants it to be, his voice is a tremendous instrument.

Anxious rasps and hoarse whispers, it sounds real and right—Woody Guthrie whipped, busted, bitter, bloody, unbowed. From his early, journalistic "protest" songs to his mid-period psychological investigations (Dylan also managed to write the best kiss-off song ever—"Positively Fourth Street"—and "Like a Rolling Stone," arguably the best rock song ever) to his current hash of gospel, blues, and pumped-up pop, Dylan has always found a distinctive sound.

Maybe he doesn't write collections of songs like *Blonde on Blonde* anymore. After Elvis Presley, who never wrote a song, there is no other American rock 'n' roll figure who comes even close to matching Dylan's Promethean contribution to the modern American pop sensibility. He is on the same trajectory as Whitman and e.e. cummings, as Wallace Stevens and Kerouac and Allen Ginsberg, as Andy Warhol—another howling, thwarted, damaged outsider's voice from the American hinterland.

His lyrics were serious, adult stuff; until Dylan, rock 'n' roll had been an unabashedly juvenile form. And while it would be wrong to call Dylan a poet, he is as important as any poet this country has produced in this century, and they will be playing his songs a century from now. Dylan remade rock 'n' roll into a viable vehicle for serious adults and remade himself into a character as compelling as Huckleberry Finn. Critics invariably fail to explain Dylan because Dylan is smarter than they are. Genius has its own alchemy; you don't break it down with a centrifuge and solvents.

●　　●　　●

The last time I saw Dylan was at the Concert for the Rock and Roll Hall of Fame in Cleveland; he wore a rock star's gold lamé shirt (and in doing so came closer than anyone else involved in that weird event to actually invoking the ghost of Elvis Presley) and muttered his way through a ragged electric set. He played electric guitar mathematically, finding the proper box and poking his fingers at the strings. He did "All Along the Watchtower" and made it sound like a tribute to Jimi Hendrix. He even deigned to speak to the audience, something he doesn't do much anymore.

"Let me hear you say *'Broooooce,'*" he urged before bringing on Bruce Springsteen, with whom he sang "Forever Young."

It wasn't the greatest performance, but it was earnest, and when Dylan stepped away from the mike to let Springsteen take a verse, a vague glimmer of a smile as brief and blue as cigarette smoke trembled on his lips.

And Dylan, child of Dylan, induced a generous impulse: one that commanded "leave him alone, he looks happy."

(1995)

The Shortstop's Son

Had my father lived, he would be sixty years old this month.

That does not seem so old to me now. It seems a perfectly reasonable attainable age, an age when one should perhaps have most things worked out. I wish my father had reached it, that he was still available for a round of golf or a quiet drink. I wish he hadn't died young thirteen years ago and that he could know me as an adult, with a mortgage and a sensible car that starts. I wish I could know him how he would have been, had he not died.

Maybe it is terrible that people die, but they do. And if my father's dying young was a tragedy, it was no more than what most people go through. I miss my father, and I often dream of him and wake up disappointed that he is not still here. It is not something you argue though, all of our fathers die and we all go on.

I do not remember any awful arguments or occasions of embarrassment; my father was a quiet man, at least with me. He was firm and he was proud and I know we argued about things that make no difference now, but even at the height of my adolescent confusion we were never estranged for more than a day or so. He was a good father and I imagine I was a good son—I did not cause him to fret; I was always able to keep my secrets secret.

He was a ballplayer, a good one, a professional for a while. He was a shortstop, a compact quick man with thick forearms. Somewhere in my mother's house there is an old scrapbook—begun by my father's mother—filled with newspaper clippings of his pro career, which was really over before I was born. Somewhere there is a photograph of him shaking hands across second base with a young Henry Aaron. Surprisingly, he hit home runs and ran well.

I don't need to look at the clipping to know how well he threw.

My father played ball all his life, until the cancer spread from his lymph nodes and through his body. I remember how he played and I even played on a few teams—in pick-up games and softball leagues—with him. I close my eyes and I can see him at shortstop, stretching across his body and picking the ball—Melville white—out of the fine dust. Now he plants his right foot and looks down into his glove as if he has discovered something exquisite and mysterious. Now he holds it in his meat hand for a split second, examining the seams. He holds it longer than is necessary. Now he fits it to his meat hand and, finally, he throws. Hard.

The base runner is invariably and inarguably out. The margin is thin, but apparent.

Some people didn't like the way my father seemed to hold the ball for a fraction of a second; they thought it something of a "hot dog" play, designed to embarrass the base runner. But it was a habit my father learned young and could never break. He simply had that kind of arm.

Sometimes when we played together—I was a shortstop, too, but not like him—they'd put me at first base. I would have to catch those balls he threw across the diamond. They would seem to rise, jumping up six inches in the last few feet before they arrived. A face-high softball six feet from the bag would end up stuck in the webbing of my glove at the top of my extension. I would feel the tug in my triceps as it slapped in; I would hold on and the runner would be out.

My father threw a live ball. And he kept his arm for a while after the chemotherapy robbed him of his hair. I remember a few weeks where he was bald but otherwise strong, when he put on a cap and went out and played shortstop in an industrial softball league. I have one of the balls from that game in my office at home.

●　　●　　●

I told no one at the newspaper I worked for that my father was dying. It was none of their business, and it was an awkward fact to work into conversation. In those days I was a police reporter and I lived in the raw way some young men do. I worked mainly at night and in the early morning. I spent my afternoons at the hospital, then I would go home to an under-furnished apartment and pass out on a futon in front of a campfire color TV, rising after a couple of hours to do my rounds and drink cop-shop coffee with detectives in polyester sport coats. It seems I never dreamed in those days; my sleep had an unhealthy, alcoholic quality.

But there were days when I didn't go to my father's bedside. Sometimes I left work and went to the library and read magazines all afternoon. Sometimes I went to the movies and sat in the cool dark. I must have forgotten my dying father a hundred times in those few months that he was hospitalized.

My father died on a Monday morning.

I only know that it was a Monday because normally it would have been one of my days off. But for some reasons I was working that Monday morning. It was odd. I had just got back to the office, after sweeping through my rounds, talking baseball with the sheriff's deputies. There was a pink phone memo on my desk; my uncle had called from the hospital. I didn't need to return the call. I typed up three briefs, hit the necessary computer keys to move them to the desk, and told the city editor I was leaving, that my father had just died.

He looked up with tender bovine eyes and nodded, and I left.

I remember the slap of my rubber-soled deck shoes in the slick waxed hallways, astringent smells of the cancer ward, the bland smiling indifference of nurses used to death, and the damnable patience of doctors. I remember molded plastic dining trays that reeked of hot water.

I remember the relief, the feeling of being done with something, and a hot viscous pounding behind my eyes. I remember the body, the blankness of the sheets, the darkening repose setting on my dead father's face. His body looked vacated. There were moans seeping through the hospital walls. I remember thinking a hospital was a bad place to die, surrounded by the muted hum of daytime soaps and pitiable noises of the infirm.

For a long time, I sat beside the corpse. I was brittle and tearless then, but if I think about it for too long now my eyes soften and get moist. There are times his absence burns and other times it seems like a dull hollowness, but mostly it is all right. I loved my father and he knew it, and I know he loved me, too. I don't think he ever despaired of me and I am glad of that. I think he trusted and respected me, that he was fairly confident that I would not disgrace myself.

And there are times I catch myself in some vocal tic of his, or the light will slant right and in a mirror I'll recognize the part of him that is me. He would be sixty now and I cannot quite imagine that, just as I cannot quite imagine that he is gone.

Sometimes I still hear him. Sometimes he is here.

(1996)